山川异域 风月同天

福州开元寺与七位日本历史文化名人

释本性 编著

宗教文化出版社

图书在版编目（CIP）数据

山川异域 风月同天：福州开元寺与七位日本历史文化名人／释本性编著．
-- 北京 ： 宗教文化出版社，2023.1
ISBN 978-7-5188-1381-0

Ⅰ．①山… Ⅱ．①释… Ⅲ．①佛教－寺庙－史料
－福州市 Ⅳ．① B947.257.1

中国国家版本馆 CIP 数据核字（2023）第 024730 号

山川异域 风月同天

——福州开元寺与七位日本历史文化名人

释本性 编著

出版发行：宗教文化出版社

地　　址：北京市西城区后海北沿 44 号（100009）

电　　话：64095215（发行部）　　64095265（编辑部）

责任编辑：王志宏

版式设计：贺　兵

印　　刷：河北信瑞彩印刷有限公司

版权专有　　侵权必究

版本记录：787 毫米×1092 毫米　16 开　7.75 印张　200 千字
　　　　　2024 年 4 月第 1 版　2024 年 4 月第 1 次印刷

书　　号：ISBN 978-7-5188-1381-0

定　　价：58.00 元

目　录 | CONTENTS

山川异域，风月同天

——福州开元寺与七位日本历史文化名人

2021 年，福州开元寺"日本空海大师和圆珍大师纪念馆"开建了！

中国外交部长王毅曾指出："纵观整个人类文明史，中日两个国家、两个民族的人文交流历时之久、规模之大、范围之广、影响之深实属罕见。这种深厚的渊源积淀了两国独特的文化交融。中日两国人民在绵延千年的历史交往中互学互鉴，兼容并蓄，相得益彰。遣隋使、遣唐使远渡重洋，全面学习借鉴中国的典章制度。鉴真、隐元东渡弘法，空海、最澄入唐请益，汉传佛教的精髓绵延至今。"①

为了让大家更详细地了解福州开元寺与日本悠远、绵长、深入、丰富的友好交往史，续写新时代中日两国友谊的新篇章，笔者特整理编撰了这本《山川异域 风月同天——福州开元寺与七位日本历史文化名人》小书，以满足大家的需要。

---

① 中华人民共和国中央人民政府网 https://www.gov.cn/guowuyuan/2019-11/25/content_5455481.htm，《王毅同日本外相茂木敏充共同主持中日高级别人文交流磋商机制首次会议》，2019-11-25，来源：新华社。

福州开元寺，福州现存最古老寺院，位于灵芝之山，称龙兴之地，历史上中国十大名寺之一，至今已走过 1500 年左右的历史，是古城福州的见证，以其深厚且著名的四大文化，即冶铸文化、海丝文化、医药文化、佛教文化，而闻名遐迩。

寺院内矗立的千年大铁佛，是中国历史全盛时期冶铁铸造业的代表遗存，更是中国佛教中心从中原转向东南沿海的象征，举世无双。

为了保护大铁佛，1997 年，在时任福建省委副书记习近平的协调和督导下，原设于寺庙之内的五金厂，无条件搬迁，开元寺进入了快速发展期。①

2002 年，时任福建省省长的习近平同志为《福州古厝》一书撰写了序言，其中说到："当我们来到开元寺，它正自豪得意地向我们表述，大铁

_____

① 出自中央电视台纪录片频道《福州古厝》第 1 集第 35 分钟。

佛是我们的先人掌握高超的冶铸技术的证明——古建筑有着丰富的人文内涵。"[①]

自唐代以来，福州开元寺作为接待外国僧侣的官方驿站，迎来了来自印度、日本、朝鲜等国的高僧、名人，其中以日本为最多。如唐代有日本真言宗创始人空海大师、遣唐大使藤原葛野麻吕、书法巨匠橘逸势、天台宗寺门派宗祖圆珍大师等；宋代有日本东大寺重建圣人重源上人、律宗戒光寺派开山祖师昙照律师、诗僧庆政上人等。

北宋时期，福州开元寺用近 50 年的时间，刊刻雕印了佛教全集，即《毗卢大藏经》，这是中国印刷史与佛教刻经史的标志性文化工程。《毗卢大藏经》先后由入宋日僧重源上人、昙照律师、庆政上人、行一、明仁等携回日本。

明末清初，渡日高僧隐元禅师的高徒，出家于福清黄檗山万福禅寺的也懒性圭禅师（？—1664），曾在福州开元寺修行并阅读《毗卢大藏经》，后来他东渡日本，不幸在途中遇风暴圆寂。之后，隐元禅师率徒应请东渡日本，赢得当时的天皇及幕府将军的尊重与支持，在京都府宇治郡开辟黄檗山万福禅寺，如今法脉绵延，黄檗宗子孙满堂，圆满了也懒性圭禅师的心愿。

二十世纪初叶，日本著名佛教学者常盘大定，五次来华实地考察佛教遗迹，尤其注重对史迹的拍摄、拓制和记录。他在中国搜集大量佛、道、儒资料，作实证研究，著有《中国佛教史迹》《中国佛教研究》《中国佛教和儒教道教》，并与关野贞合写《中国文化史迹》十二卷，享誉海内外。

---

① 习近平：《福州古厝序》，《人民日报》2019 年 6 月 8 日。

其中第五次考察以闽粤两地的古寺为中心，他也曾到福州开元寺拍摄、记录，为大铁佛留下了珍贵的影像资料。

改革开放后，自福州开元寺开始恢复为宗教活动场所，到福州开元寺访问、参拜的日本各界团体与个人，年复一年，从未停歇。如 2004 年，日本高野山真言宗宗务总长生土川正道长老率日本真言宗佛教代表团一行 300 多人访寺，隆重祭拜宗祖空海大师圣像。

近年来更是络绎不绝。如 2017 年 9 月，以原日本国众议院议员冈下信子女士为代表的日本议员友好访问团，参访福州开元寺。

2017 年 12 月，日本执政党之自民党干事长二阶俊博先生与公明党干事长井上义久先生一行 30 余人，在中共中央联络部宋涛部长的陪同下，到访开元寺，朝礼空海大师、圆珍大师圣像及法身塔，于空海纪念堂空海大师圣像前上香礼拜，并于寺中与宋涛部长、笔者一同种下桂花树，祝福中日友谊之树常青。

2019 年 4 月，日本驻广州总领事石塚英树到访福州开元寺。

2019 年 7 月，日本驻华大使横井裕先生夫妇一行莅寺，于空海大师圣像前上香，对福州开元寺与日本的深厚历史渊源，赞叹不已。

2019 年 8 月，以日本公明党代理干事长兼国际委员会委员长、众议员远山清彦为团长的日本超党派年轻政治家代表团一行 11 人到访福州开元寺，

2019 年 9 月，日本长崎县知事中村法道等日本友好人士一行，访问福州开元寺。

2019 年 11 月，日本著名导演、编剧、第 81 届奥斯卡金像奖最佳外语

片获得者泷田洋二郎先生一行访问福州开元寺，泷田洋二郎先生于开元寺的药师如来、千年铁佛、空海大师坐像前虔诚礼拜上香、供奉三宝，并表达了此次来到开元寺的欢喜和愉快。

2021 年 11 月，日本驻华大使垂秀夫走访福州开元寺，并赠送他的摄影作品予开元寺留念。

以下我们为大家详细介绍，唐宋时期到福州开元寺居住或参访、学习的 7 位日本历史文化名人。

山川、域を異にすれども、
風月、天を同じゅうす

──福州開元寺と七人の日本歴史文化有名人

　2021 年、福州開元寺の「日本空海大師と円珍大師記念館」がオープンした。

　中国国務委員兼外交部長の王毅氏が次のように指摘していた。人類文明史を伺っても、中日両国、両民族のように、長期にわたり、大規模且つ広範囲で、深い影響をもたらした人文・文化交流はまれに見ることである。中日両国の人文交流は根源が深く、両国の独特の文化的融合を蓄積した。中日両国民が何千年にわたる悠久の交流史があり、互いに学び合い、参考にし合い、異なったものを受け入れて、それぞれの発展を促進した。遣隋使、遣唐使が海をわたり、中国の経典・制度を全面的に学び、参考した。鑑真、隠元は日本に渡航して付法し、空海、最澄は唐の国から制度・文物を導入して、漢伝仏教の真髄は今日まで伝わってきた。

　福州開元寺と日本の間の悠遠且つ恒久的で、深刻且つ豊富的な交流史を詳しく紹介し、引き続き中日両国友情の新時代を開くために、福州

開元寺は小冊子「山川、域を異にすれども、風月、天を同じゅうす――福州開元寺と日本歴史文化有名人」を編著し、皆様の需要に応える。

　福州開元寺は、福州市に現存する最古の寺院であり、「竜興の地」と呼ばれた霊芝の山に位置し、中国歴史上十代名刹の一つである。約1500年の歴史を持つ開元寺は、古都福州を見守りながら、冶金鋳造文化、海上シルクロード文化、医薬文化、仏教文化という深厚な「四大文化」で名を馳せている。

　境内にそびえ立つ千年大鉄仏は、中国歴史全盛期に発達した鋳鉄業を代表する無二の遺作であり、中国仏教の中心地が中原から東南沿岸部に移転する象徴でもある。

　大鉄仏を保護するために、1997年、その時福建省委副書記を務めた習近平氏の調整と指導によって、境内にある金属工場が無条件で撤廃され、開元寺が急速発展期を迎えた。

　2002年、その時福建省省長を務めた習近平氏が『福州古厝』という本の序文を作成し、次のように書いた。我々が開元寺にやってくると、大鉄仏は先人たちが把握した優れた冶金鋳造技術を証明し、歴史的建造物は豊かな人文内容を包含していることを我々に誇らしく伝わってきた。

　唐の時代から、福州開元寺は外国人僧侶を応接する公式宿駅として、インド、日本、朝鮮諸国からの高僧や名人を迎えていた。その中で、日本からの人数が最も多いとされていた。例えば、唐の時代に、日本真言宗開祖の空海大師、遣唐大使の藤原葛野麻呂、書道巨匠の橘逸

勢、天台宗寺門派開祖の円珍大師などが数えられ、宋の時代に、日本東大寺再興聖人の重源上人、律宗戒光寺派開祖の曇照律師、詩僧の慶政上人などが数えられる。

北宋の時代、福州開元寺は50年近くをかけて、仏教全集「毘盧大蔵経」を彫刻印刷した。これは中国印刷史と仏教刻経史をマークした文化プロジェクトである。「毘盧大蔵経」は前後、宋に来た日本僧侶の重源上人、曇照律師、慶政上人、行一、明仁によって日本に持ち帰られていた。

明末清初、渡日高僧隠元禅師の一番弟子である、福清黄檗山万福禅寺に出家した也懶性圭禅師（？～1664）は、福州開元寺で修行し、「毘盧大蔵経」を読んだことがある。日本に渡ろうとする途中、暴風雨に遭難し入寂した。その後、隠元禅師が日本からの招請に応じて弟子を伴って東渡して、当時の天皇及び幕府将軍の崇敬と支持を得て、京都府宇治

郡に黄檗山萬福寺を開創した。大法は永々脈々と受け継がれ今日に至り、黄檗宗の信者は輩出し、也懶性圭禅師の願いを叶えただろう。

二十世紀初期、日本著名な仏教学者常磐大定は、5度にわたり訪中し、各地の仏教史跡を調査し、とりわけ史跡の撮影、採拓、記録に携わっていた。中国で、仏教・道教・儒教に関する資料を大量に調査し、実証研究に取り組み、『中国仏教史蹟』六冊、『中国仏教の研究』、『中国における仏教と儒教・道教』を著わし、関野貞と『中国文化史蹟』十二巻を共著し、国内外に知れ渡っていた。五回目の調査は福建省と広東省両地の古寺をめぐるゆえに、福州開元寺に訪ねて撮影、記録したことがあり、大鉄仏の貴重な画像映像資料を残していた。

改革開放後、福州開元寺は宗教活動場所として再開し、ここに来て訪問、参拝する日本各界の団体や個人は年を重ねて後を絶たない。例えば、2004年、日本高野山真言宗宗務総長生土川正道長老をはじめ、日本真言宗仏教代表団一行300人が寺に訪れ、丁寧に重々しく宗祖空海大師の聖像を拝観した。

近年の交流も絶え間なく続いている。例えば、2017年9月、日本衆議院元議員岡下信子をはじめとする日本議員友好訪問団が福州開元寺を訪れた。

2017年12月、日本与党自民党総幹事長の二階俊博先生及び公明党幹事長の井上義久先生一行30人は、中共中央連絡部部長の宋涛先生が伴って、開元寺を訪問した。空海大師、円珍大師の聖像及び法身塔に参詣し、空海記念堂にある空海大師の聖像にお線香を供えて参拝するだけ

でなく、宋涛部長、本性住持と一緒に、末永い中日友好を祝福して金木犀の木を植樹した。

2019年4月、在広州日本国総領事館の石塚英樹総領事が福州開元寺を訪問した。

2019年7月、日本駐中国大使横井裕先生ご夫婦一行は福州開元寺を訪問し、空海大師の聖像前にお線香を供え、福州開元寺と日本との深い歴史的根源に驚嘆した。

2019年8月、日本公明党幹事長代理兼国際委員会委員長、衆議院議員の遠山清彦を団長とする日本超党派若手政治家代表団一行11人が福州開元寺を訪問した。

2019年9月、日本長崎県知事中村法道をはじめとする日本友好人士一行が福州開元寺を訪問した。

2019年11月、日本名監督、脚本家、第81回アカデミー外国映画賞受賞者滝田洋二郎一行が福州開元寺を訪問した。滝田洋二郎が薬師如来、千年鉄仏、空海大師坐像の前にお線香を供えて礼拝し、三宝さまを供養した上で、開元寺訪問の喜びと楽しみを表していた。

2021年11月、日本の中国駐在大使である垂秀夫は福州の開元寺を訪れ、自身の写真作品を記念品として開元寺に贈呈した。

これより、唐と宋の時代に、福州開元寺に滞在したり、訪問したり、修行したりした7名の日本歴史文化有名人を紹介する。

（訳者　顧碩）

Lands Apart, Sky Shared

Fuzhou Kaiyuan Temple and Seven Japanese Historical and Cultural Figures

In 2021, the Memorial Hall of Master Kūkai and Master Enchin has begun construction at Fuzhou Kaiyuan Temple.

China's State Councilor and Foreign Minister Wang Yi previously noted that, "Throughout the human history, cultural exchanges between China and Japan or their peoples are actually very special in terms of the long time span, large scale, broad scope and profound influence. Such historical linkages have been strongly promoting the cross–fertilization of cultures. The two peoples have shared experience and learned from each other over the past thousand years, creating an inclusive and welcoming environment for cultural exchanges. During that period, Japanese missions to Sui China or Tang China traveled across vast oceans for a comprehensive learning of China's institutional systems. Japanese Buddhist monks like Kūkai and Saichō came to Tang China to learn more about Buddhism; while Chinese Buddhist monks like Jianzhen and Yinyuan sailed east to propagate Buddhism to the Japanese. These valuable cultural exchanges make the essence of Han Buddhism or Chinese Buddhism still shine today."

The book *Lands Apart, Sky Shared: Fuzhou Kaiyuan Temple and Seven Japanese Historical and Cultural Figures* was specially compiled for the purpose of providing more detailed information on the long-term close and profound relations between Japan and the temple, and of strengthening Sino-Japanese ties in the new era.

Situated on Mount Lingzhi (also known as the Cultural Origin of Fuzhou) , Fuzhou Kaiyuan Temple, which was built about 1,500 year ago, is the oldest extant temple in Fuzhou. As a witness to the rich history of Fuzhou, it once ranked among the top ten temples in the country. The temple has now been renowned for its profound and eminent culture related to the metal smelting and casting, the Maritime Silk Road, the Bhaisajyaguru Buddha (Medicine Buddha) and the Buddhism.

The remarkable iron Amitābha Buddha statue at the temple, which traces back over one thousand years ago, is regarded as a representative work of China's advanced iron smelting and casting skills, and marks the shifting of China's Buddhist center from the Central Plain (Zhongyuan) to Southeast China.

In 1997, under the auspices and coordination of President Xi Jinping, then Deputy Secretary of CPC Fujian Provincial Committee, the hardware factory in Fuzhou Kaiyuan Temple was relocated for better protection of the Great Buddha statue without preconditions. Since then, Fuzhou Kaiyuan Temple has entered a period of rapid development.

In 2002, President Xi, then governor of Fujian Province, wrote in the preface for *Ancient Buildings in Fuzhou*, "Fuzhou Kaiyuan Temple has proudly shown the world that its iron Great Buddha statue demonstrates our ancestors' excellence in metal smelting and casting and that ancient buildings reflect the richness of culture".

Since the Tang dynasty, Fuzhou Kaiyuan Temple had served as the official posthouse where monks from India, Japan, Korea and other countries were received, with Japanese being the largest group, including the Master Kūkai（Founder of Japanese Shingon Buddhism）, the Envoy Fujiwara no Kadanomaro, the Great Calligrapher Tachibana no Hayanari, the Master Enchin（Founder of the Jimon School of Tendai Buddhism）who visited China during the Tang dynasty, and the Great Monk Chōgen（Daikanjin of Tōdaiji Temple）, the Risshū Monk Donsho Ninritsu（Founder of Kaikouji Temple in Japan）and the Monk–Poet Keisei who visited China during the Song dynasty.

During the Northern Song dynasty, Fuzhou Kaiyuan Temple spent nearly 50 years to engrave and print a complete collection of Buddhist scriptures, namely the Pilu Tripitaka, which is considered as a significant cultural project in the history of Chinese printing and of Buddhist scriptures engraving. Then the Pilu Tripitaka was introduced to Japan by the Japanese Monk Chōgen, the Risshū Monk Donsho Ninritsu, the Monk-Poet Keisei, Gyouichi and Meijin.

Yinyuan or Ingen Ryūki was one of the most prominent Chinese monks who journeyed to Japan. In the late Ming and early Qing dynasties, one of Yinyuan's eminent disciples named Shokei Yaran (?-1664) practiced Buddhism and studied the Pilu Tripitaka at Fuzhou Kaiyuan Temple. Yaran entered the religous life at Wanfu Temple on Mount Huangbo in Fuqing, Fujian Province. Unfortunately, he was killed in a shipwreck on his way to Japan. At the request of Japanese monks, Yinyuan and his disciples later went to Japan, which won the respect and support of the then Japanese emperor and the then shōgun (the military dictator of Japan). In Uji, Kyoto, Yinyuan established the Manpukuji Temple. It is the head temple of the Japanese Ōbaku Zen sect, named after the Wanfu Temple. There are now many monks practicing the doctrines of the Ōbaku Zen sect, which has fulfilled Shokei Yaran's wishes.

In the early twentieth century, famous Japanese Buddhist scholar Daijo Tokiwa paid five visits to China to explore the Buddhist relics there. He spent lots of time photographing, documenting and making rubbings of the relics. He also collected material on Buddhism, Taoism, and Confucianism in China for conducting empirical researches. Daijo Tokiwa wrote six volumes of *Historical Relics of Chinese Buddhism, Studies in Chinese Buddhism* and *Buddhism in China in its Relation to Confucianism and Taoism*. He has co-written with Tadashi Sekino twelve volumes of *Chinese Cultural Heritage*, which is well-known at home and abroad. During his fifth visit to China, he focused on the ancient temples in Fujian and Guangdong Provinces. He also went to Fuzhou Kaiyuan Temple and took many photos and videos, including videos on the iron Great Buddha statue there.

After China's reform and opening-up, Fuzhou Kaiyuan Temple began to be used again as a place for religious ceremonies and practices. Every year, many Japanese groups and individuals from all walks of life visited the temple. In 2004, Shodo Habukawa, in charge of the religious affairs of Koyasan Shingon Buddhism in Japan, led a delegation of more than 300 people to visit the temple and pray in front of Kūkai's statue there.

Over recent years, more and more Japanese people have come to visit Fuzhou Kaiyuan temple. In September 2017, a delegation of the House of Representatives of Japan, headed by former Representative Ms. Nobuko Okashita, paid a friendly visit to the temple.

In December 2017, a group of more than 30 people, including Mr. Toshihiro Nikai, Secretary General of Japan's governing Liberal Democratic Party, and Mr. Yoshihisa Inoue, then Secretary General of Japan's Komeito Party, visited the temple. They were accompanied by Mr. Song Tao, head of the International Liaison Department of the Communist Party of China. The group prayed in front of the statues of Kūkai and Enchin and stupas representing their Dharmakayas（body of essence）. They prayed and burned incense sticks in front of Kūkai's statue at the Memorial Hall of Kūkai. They also planted Osmanthus Fragrans in the temple with Song Tao and the Abbot Benxing of the temple to bless the friendship between China and Japan.

In April 2019, Mr. Hideki Ishizuka, Consul General of Japan in Guangzhou, visited the temple.

In July 2019, Mr. Yutaka Yokoi, Ambassador of Japan to China, and his wife visited the temple and burned incense sticks in front of Kūkai's statue, marveling at the profound historical ties between Japan and the temple.

In August 2019, a non-partisan delegation of 11 young Japanese politicians visited the temple. The group was headed by Mr. Kiyohiko Toyama, Acting Chief General and Chairman of International Commission of the Komeito Party, and member of the House of Representatives of Japan.

In September 2019, a Japanese group including Mr. Hōdō Nakamura, governor of Nagasaki Prefecture, visited the temple.

In November 2019, Mr. Yōjirō Takita visited the temple. He is a famous Japanese director, screenwriter, and the winner of the Best Foreign Language Film at the 81st Academy Awards. He prayed in front of the statues of Bhaisajyaguru Buddha, thousand-year-old iron Amitābha Buddha and Kūkai.

He also burned incense sticks, piously worshiped the Triratna（Three Jewels）, and expressed joy and happiness about the visit.

In November 2021, Japanese Ambassador to China, Chui Hideo, visited Kaiyuan Temple in Fuzhou and presented his photographic works as a souvenir to the temple.

The following is a detailed description of the seven Japanese historical and cultural figures who visited or lived at Fuzhou Kaiyuan Temple to study Buddhism during the Tang and Song dynasties.

（Translated by Pan Lin）

日本真言宗开山祖师

——空海大师

空海大师（774—835），俗姓佐伯，幼名真鱼，后亦名遍照金刚、弘法大师。出生于日本赞岐国多度郡屏风浦（今香川县善通寺市），一个当地的名门望族——佐伯家族，父亲是郡里衙门的官员。其舅舅是日本第五十代天皇桓武天皇的皇子伊予亲王的侍讲，即皇子的老师，回乡省亲时见外甥聪慧异常，就经常教授空海学习儒家经典等。

日本延历七年（788），舅舅带着他一起来到当时的新都长冈京（现在的京都府向日市）。延历十年（791），进入当时培养官吏的教育机关"大学寮"

明经科，学习《书经》《诗经》《左传》等汉典，空海 18 岁时即发表《聋瞽指归》，后易名为《三教指归》，申学道之志。后遇僧侣授予"虚空藏菩萨求闻持法"，豁然开朗，于是一心向佛。延历十四年（795），空海 22 岁时，在奈良东大寺戒坛院受戒成为正式僧侣，改名为空海。

大唐贞元二十年（804），三十多岁的空海随遣唐使入华求法。船只在途中被风暴吹离航道，漂至福州长溪赤岸（今福建霞浦）。因国书等凭证并不在这艘船上，难以取信于当地守官，紧急关头，空海代遣唐大使藤原葛野麻吕向福建主官致书《为大使与福州观察使书》，其纯正的汉文、充足的理由、诚恳的情意，打动了刚上任的福建观察使阎济美，他们终于被允许登岸，并被护送入住福州开元寺。

在福州开元寺居住时，空海与寺僧惠灌等结下了深厚的友谊。四十九年后，空海大师的侄女之子圆珍入唐求法，也曾居住于福州开元寺，惠灌法师时任方丈，他向圆珍打听空海的近况，得知空海大师已经圆寂，惠灌法师流泪悲叹说：不能再和空海切磋交流了。圆珍大师后来在书中记载了此事。

在福州开元寺期间，空海大师还作了一首《灵源深处离合诗》，诗云："磴危人难行，石巇兽无升，烛暗迷前后，蜀人不得过。"如今，福州开元寺内的灵源阁依然耸立。

空海大师因随身无官方文书又系私费留学僧，本不能入京，于是他在开元寺又写了《请福州观察使入京》，再次投书福建观察使，恳请入京。《灵源深处离合诗》《为大使与福州观察使书》《请福州观察使入京》三篇作品成为流传千余年的文宝。

遍照發揮性靈集序
西山禪念沙門真濟撰集
余少小也顧貴先此之鳳志學之後樂寂歷
不屑此事仰淘人之幽行聊大道之大妙炎
有一上人觀曰大遍照金剛青懿摘秘林之
春藜豁桹富山河之藜辛逐則陋域中近智
蔡超然遠歲出俗入真去偈嚴轄淡之英
柿木靈草之區耳目所經未嘗不宛每嘆曰

高野山萬燈會願文一首
勸進奉造佛塔知識書一首
遍照發揮性靈集卷第八目錄終

遍照發揮性靈集補闕鈔卷第八
大夫笠左衛佐爲亡室遺大日摜像願文
恭聞寶日曜世者智珠斜照也者理智能照
物有功理即攝摎無亂捕敀故大身孕法界
而無外光默攺廣心吞蒼空以無中理智非
知即我身心也三自法界者迷蒙也
達塵體之不二覺滔心之如一所謂我大師
薄伽梵尚毘盧遮那蓮他世揭多其人也

遍照發揮性靈集卷第七目錄

在获得朝廷允许其进京的批文后，空海北上长安，入住西明寺。他博览内经外典，遍访诸寺名僧，805年5月下旬，往谒唐密法脉传人惠果大师于青龙寺东塔院，请求传法。惠果大师喜道："吾待汝久，来何迟矣。"空海从惠果大师受胎藏界和金刚界曼荼罗法，并受传法阿阇黎的灌顶。当年年底，惠果大师圆寂，空海奉唐宪宗命，撰写碑文。一个入唐学法才半年的外国留学生，能得到为惠果大师这样的大祖师写碑铭的荣耀，可见空海当时的修行成就已经不同寻常。

唐元和元年（806），空海搭乘遣唐使判官高阶远成的船回到日本，带回了大量经卷、佛像、法器，仅佛典即达200多部，500多卷。他后来撰写了《御请来目录》，列出长长目录清单，上奏天皇。

空海离唐前，平时交游的好友，僧人昙靖、鸿渐，士官文人朱千乘、朱少端、郑壬等，纷纷赠诗送别。郑壬称空海为"异才"，赠诗云："承化来中国，朝天是外臣，异才谁作侣，孤屿自为邻。雁塔归殊域，鲸波涉巨津，他年续僧史，更载一贤人。"预言空海将来必载入史册。

空海归国第二年，在奈良久米寺开始讲授《大日经》。大同三年（808），敕许弘通真言宗。大同四年（809），入宫说法。弘仁元年（810），在高雄山寺开坛弘法。接受灌顶者，上自嵯峨天皇、名僧最澄，下至黎民百姓，不计其数。

816年空海于纪伊（今和歌山县）开创高野山，号金刚峰寺。823年诏赐京都东寺为密教永久根本道场。"东密"名称即由此而来。曾兼任东大寺别当，统辖一寺僧职，补大僧正位。

公元835年，空海大师圆寂。嵯峨上皇作悼亡诗《哭海上人》。后来

天皇赐谥"弘法大师"。

空海大师是杰出的宗教家、书法家、文学家、教育家。他善于诗文书画，尤以书法精妙。空海大师对汉字之篆、隶、真、行、草五体皆精通，唐德宗授予其"五笔和尚"的雅号，在日本有"草圣"之称，与嵯峨天皇以及一同留学归来的橘逸势被合称为日本"书道三笔"。空海大师还根据汉字草书发展完善了日本文字平假名，由此有了今天的日本文字。

此外，空海大师在教育等方面也贡献良多，他仿照唐朝在日本设立综艺种智院，招请老师讲授佛教以及儒道的内容，对于后世教育的发展起到很大的作用。

空海大师之著作极丰，教义方面有《辩显密二教论》《秘藏宝钥》《十住心论》《付法传》《即身成佛义》《吽字义》《般若心经秘键》等，文学方面有《文镜秘府论》《文笔眼心钞》《性灵集》等。

霞浦赤岸被称为空海大师"入唐初地"，福州开元寺被称为空海大师"入唐首刹"，现有日本佛教界赠送安奉的空海大师入唐之地碑、空海大师立像、空海大师坐像、空海大师法身塔、中日友谊树等，福州开元寺还为纪念空海大师入唐居住该寺这一段历史，设立了空海大师纪念堂。作为大师入唐驻锡首刹，又是日本佛教真言宗祖庭，每年都有不少日本各界人士与真言宗僧俗，前来福州开元寺参观、朝拜。

日本真言宗開祖

——空海大師

　　空海大師（774—835）、俗姓佐伯氏、幼名を真魚といい、後に遍照金剛、弘法大師ともいう。日本讃岐国多度郡屏風浦（現在香川県善通寺市）の豪族、郡役所役人の佐伯氏の子として生まれた。日本第五十代桓武天皇の皇子の教育係を務めた伯父は帰省時、空海の才能を見抜き、儒教経典などを教えていた。

　　日本延歴7年（788）、空海が伯父に連れられて当時の新都長岡京（現在京都区向日市）にやってきた。延歴10年（791）、空海は官吏養成機関「大学寮」明経科に入って、『書経』『詩経』『左伝』などの漢籍・詩文を勉強した。18歳の時に、『聾瞽指帰』を書き、更にそれを『三教指帰』に再編し、出家の志を表明した。その後、一人の僧侶から「虚空蔵菩薩求聞持法」を学び、仏道に進む決心を固めた。延歴14年（795）、22歳の空海は、奈良の東大寺戒壇院で受戒をして正式に僧侶になり、「空海」に改名した。

　　唐の貞元20年（804）、三十代の空海は遣唐使船に乗り、唐の国を目指した。ところが嵐に遭い、大きく航路を外れた船は福州長渓赤岸（現在福建の霞浦）に漂着した。空海を乗せた船に、正式な使節である

ことを証明する国書などがないために、役人に信用されず、一行の上陸
も許されなかった。危機一髪の際、空海大師が遣唐大使の藤原葛野麻呂
に代わって福建の役人に向けて『大使、福州ノ観察使ニ与フル為ノ書』
を書きました。その壮麗な漢文章、整然とした理由と真摯な情は、福州
の観察使閻済美を感動させた。その後、上陸が許可され、福州開元寺ま
で護衛して宿泊させた。

　福州開元寺に滞在した時、空海大師は僧侶の恵潅などと深い友情を
結んだ。四十九年後、空海大師の姪の息子である円珍が入唐求法し、福
州開元寺で滞留したことがある。当時住職を務める恵潅法師は円珍に、
「五筆和尚（空海のこと）は健在か否か」と尋ねたという。入滅したと
答えを受けた恵潅法師が、「また空海と切磋交流はできない」と涙を流
して悲嘆した。円珍はこの事を後の文書に記録した。

　福州開元寺に滞在中、空海大師はまた『霊源深処離合詩』を書い
た。詩文に、「険しい階段は人にとって登り難く、高い岩は獣さえ上が
れない。ロウソクの光は暗くて前後も見えなく、蜀の人さえ乗り越えら
れない。」と書いた。今日、福州開元寺の霊源閣は依然としてそびえ立
っている。

　空海大師は官庁文書を持っていない上に自費留学僧の身であるた
め、長安に行くことができないはずだが、開元寺で改めて福建観察使に
あてて上申書『福州ノ観察使ニ与ヘテ入京スル啓』をしたためた。『大
使、福州ノ観察使ニ与フル為ノ書』『霊源深処離合詩』『福州ノ観察使ニ
与ヘテ入京スル啓』、この三部の作品は千年あまりの歴史を経て伝わっ

てきた文化の重宝である。

　　空海大師は長安入りの批准をもらい、長安に向けて北上し、西明寺
に住していた。国内外の経典を精力的に学び、各地の寺院や名僧を訪問
していた。805 年 5 月末、青龍寺東塔院に唐代の密教継承者恵果和尚を
訪ねて、密教の伝授を受けていた。空海は恵果大師から胎蔵界と金剛界
曼荼羅大法を受け、伝法阿闍梨位の潅頂を受けた。同年年末、恵果大師
入寂後、唐の憲宗皇帝に指名されて追悼の碑文を書いた。入唐してわず
か半年の一介の留学生が、恵果大師のような大祖師のために碑文を書く

ほどの名誉を取得するのは、空海大師の修行はただものではないことが伺われるだろう。

　唐の元和元年（806）、空海大師は遣唐使判官高階遠成の船に乗って日本に戻り、膨大な典籍、仏像、法具などを日本にもたらした。仏教経典だけでもその数は200部、500巻を超えた。その後、密教経典・法具などを記した『御請来目録』を天皇に奉呈した。

　空海大師は唐を離れる前に、僧侶の曇靖、鴻漸や、士官文人の朱千乗、朱少端、鄭壬など普段よく交流してきた友人たちは、それぞれ詩を歌って送別の意を表した。鄭壬は空海を「異才」を称し、「受法のため中国に来て、外国人の大臣になった。誰が異才に伴うかというと、島も自らの隣人にするのだ。雁塔（西安）から異域に帰航する時、また巨大な波に会うだろう。高僧たちを記載する歴史に、もうひとり賢人の名前を加えるべき。」という詩を贈呈し、空海は必ず歴史に残る大物になること予言した。

　空海大師は帰国後二年目、奈良の久米寺で「大日経」を伝授することを始めた。大同3年（808）、真言宗を流布する勅許を得た。大同4年（809）、朝命により上京し付法した。弘仁元年（810）、高雄山寺を本拠に布教を開始した。上は嵯峨天皇、最澄らに、下は庶民百姓に、数え切れない人たちに灌頂を授けていた。

　816年、空海大師は紀伊（現在和歌山県）で高野山を開き、金剛峰寺を建立した。823年、京都の東寺を天皇より与えられ、密教永久根本道場とされた。「東密」という名称がここから由来している。また、東

大寺別当を兼ね、僧職を統轄し、大僧正位を追贈された。

　　835 年、空海大師は入寂した。嵯峨上皇は空海の入定を哀悼し、「海上人を哭す」の詩を書いた。後に、天皇から「弘法大師」の諡号が贈られた。

　　空海大師は傑出した宗教家、書道家、文学者、教育家であり、詩文書画に精通し、とりわけ書道に造詣が深い。空海大師は漢字の篆書・隷書・真書、行書、草書と五つの書体に精通し、唐の徳宗皇帝から「五筆和尚」の雅号を贈られ、日本では「草聖」と呼ばれ、嵯峨天皇及び同じく唐に留学してきた橘逸勢とともに「書道三筆」と呼ばれた。その上、空海大師は漢字の草書によって、日本文字の平仮名を完善させ、片仮名も平仮名を基礎に徐々に形成し、今日日本の文字が形成した。

　　それに、空海大師は教育面でも大きな貢献をした。唐に模倣して日本で綜芸種智院を創立し、先生を招聘して仏教や儒教の学問を教え、後世の教育発展に大いに役立った。

　　空海大師は多くの著作を著している。教義に関しては『弁顕密二教論』『秘蔵宝鑰』『十住心論』『付法伝』『即身成仏義』『吽字義』『般若心経秘鍵』などがあり、文学に関しては『文鏡秘府論』『文筆眼心抄』『性霊集』などがある。

　　福建省の霞浦赤岸は空海大師の「入唐初地」と呼ばれ、福州開元寺は空海大師の「入唐初刹」と呼ばれ、日本仏教界から寄贈された空海大師入唐初地碑、空海大師立像、空海大師坐像、空海大師法身塔、中日友好の木などがある。福州開元寺は、空海大師が当寺に滞在した歴史を記

念するために、空海大師記念堂を設立した。福州開元寺は空海大師が入唐後最初に滞在した場所、それに日本仏教真言宗の祖庭とされ、毎年、日本からの各界人士と真言宗僧侶たちがたくさんここに来て、見学したり拝観したりしている。

Founder of Japanese Shingon Buddhism

—Master Kūkai

Master Kūkai (774–835) , who had the birth name Mao (True Fish) and the secular name Saeki no Mao, was born into the noble family of Saeki in Byōbugaura, Sanuki Province (now Zentsūji, Kagawa Prefecture) . Shingon followers usually refer to him by the honorific titles of Henjō–Kongō and Kōbō–Daishi. His father was a local government official. His maternal uncle was the teacher of Imperial Prince Iyo, son of Emperor Kanmu (the 50th Emperor of Japan) . On his family visits, he found Kūkai an intelligent boy and instructed him in the Confucian classics.

In the seventh year of the Enryaku era (788) , Kūkai traveled with his uncle to the then new capital, Nagaoka–kyō (Parts of the capital were in the present–day Mukō, Kyoto Prefecture) . In 791, he entered the Imperial university of Japan, the Daigakuryō, to study Chinese classics, such as *Book of Documents*, *Classic of Poetry*, and *Zuo Tradition*. At age 18, Kūkai published his first major work *Rōko Shiiki*, later changed its name to *Sangō Shiiki* (Essentials of the Three Teachings) , to express his aspirations for spiritual studies. Later, he met a monk who taught him Kokuzou–Gumonji (a secret doctrine method) .

He was enlightened and decided to devote himself to Buddhism. In 795, when he was 22, he was ordained in the ordination hall of Tōdaiji Temple in Nara and was given the religious name Kūkai.

In 804, in his thirties, Kūkai traveled with the Japanese mission to Tang China for studying Chinese Buddhism. His ship was blown off course by storm and arrived in Chi'an, Changxi, Fuzhou (now Xiapu, Fujian Province) . As the travel credentials were left in another ship, they could not convince the local officials to let them land. To solve this dilemma, Kūkai wrote a letter on behalf of the envoy Fujiwara no Kadanomaro to Yan Jimei, Governor of Fujian Province. The newly appointed governor was moved by his fluent Chinese writing, powerful reasoning, and sincere emotion, and allowed them to land and accommodated them at Fuzhou Kaiyuan Temple.

At the Kaiyuan Temple, Kūkai developed a close friendship with Master Huiguan. 49 years later, Master Enchin, son of Kūkai's niece, went to China and also resided at Fuzhou Kaiyuan Temple. When Master Huiguan, then abbot of the temple, asked Enchin about Kūkai and heard that Kūkai had died, he wept and sighed, "I could not discuss Buddhism with Kūkai any more." Enchin later wrote about this in his book.

During his stay at Fuzhou Kaiyuan Temple, Kūkai composed a poem called "In the Depth of Lingyuan", a Chinese acrostic poem: Stone-paved slopes crumble, they are difficult for people to traverse / The rocks are steep, wild beasts do not climb them / The torch is extinguished, there is confusion all around / People from Shu would be unable to make their way through. Nowadays, Fuzhou Kaiyuan Temple still has a pavilion (Lingyuan Ge) that shares its name with this poem.

Since Kūkai did not carry travel credentials with him and came to study at his own expense, he was not permitted to enter the capital Chang'an at the outset, so he wrote again at the Kaiyuan Temple to the Fujian Observer. His Chinese acrostic poem "In the Depth of Lingyuan" and two letters to the governor of Fuzhou were treasured as masterpieces for more than a thousand years.

When he finally got the official permission, Kūkai went north to Chang'an and resided at Ximing Temple. He studied all Chinese classics, including Buddhist canon, and visited famous monks of many temples. In late May, 805, he visited Master Huiguo, the exponent of Tángmì (Tang dynasty Esoterica) , at Qinglong Temple and asked for his instruction. Master Huiguo said in a pleased tone, "I have waited for you for a long time. Why didn't you visit me earlier?" Kūkai studied the Womb Realm Mandala and the Diamond Realm Mandala, and received the abhisheka from Master Huiguo. At the end of that year, Master Huiguo died. Kūkai was asked by Emperor Xianzong of Tang to write the tomb inscription for Master Huiguo. It was a great honor for a foreign student who had been studying in Tang China for only half a year and a proof of Kūkai's extraordinary achievement in Buddhist studies.

In the first year of the Yuanhe era (806) of the Tang dynasty, Master Kūkai arrived back to Japan on the ship of Takashina no Tonari, a Japanese envoy to Tang China. He also arrived with more than 200 Buddhist scriptures (over 500 volumes) , Buddha statues and Buddhist instruments. Master Kūkai later presented to the Japanese Emperor the *Goshorai mokuroku*, which listed the items he brought back from China.

Upon Master Kūkai leaving China for Japan, his Chinese friends composed farewell poems to convey their emotions, including monks like Tanjing and Hongjian, and literati like Zhu Qiancheng, Zhu Shaoduan and Zheng Ren. Zheng

Ren, who deemed Master Kūkai a man of "exceptional talent", wrote a poem for him. It says that Master Kūkai would remain in the pages of history: In the pursuit of Buddhist teachings, Master Kūkai came to Tang China / As a man of exceptional talent, he is matched by few / Against the wind and wave, the ship leaves Chang'an for Japan / When compiling the history of Buddhism, his name will be recorded without doubt.

A year after his return to Japan, Master Kūkai began to propagate the *Mahāvairocana Tantra* at Kumedera Temple in Nara. In the third year of the Daidō era（808）, he received a grant from the Japanese Government to propagate the Shingon Buddhism. In 809, he was invited to preach at the imperial palace. In the first year of the Kōnin era（810）, Master Kūkai moved to Takaosanji Temple, where Emperor Saga, monk Saichō and countless others underwent the abhisheka presided by Kūkai.

In 816, Master Kūkai established the ecclesiastic head temple of Koyasan Shingon Buddhism called Kongōbuji Temple, located on Mount Kōya, present-day Wakayama Prefecture. In 823, the Japanese Emperor enabled Kūkai to make Tōji Temple in Kyoto the very center of Esoteric Buddhism. Some said Eastern Esotericism was so named due to Tōji Temple（literally Eastern Temple）. Kūkai was also appointed the administrative head of Tōdaiji Temple and being considered for the rank of Daisōjō.

In 835, Master Kūkai passed away. Emperor Saga wrote a lament poem on his death and Emperor Daigo bestowed on him the posthumous title of Kōbō–

Daishi.

Master Kūkai was a religious leader, calligrapher, poet and educator. Besides, as a literary all-rounder, Master Kūkai was especially talented at Chinese calligraphy, including Zhuanshu, Lishu, Zhenshu, Xingshu and Caoshu. In Tang China, He was hailed by Emperor Dezong as the Buddhist Monk Master of Five Chinese Calligraphic Styles. In Japan, he was referred to as the Sage of Caoshu. Master Kūkai is also one of the Sanpitsu (Three Great Brushes) in Japan, alongside Emperor Saga and Tachibana no Hayanari. In addition to his role as calligrapher, Master Kūkai developed Hiragana based on Chinese grass script,

while katakana was evolved from Chinese regular script. Then Hiragana and katakana together formed the modern Japanese writing system.

Master Kūkai also contributed greatly to the education in Japan. Following the Tang China's model, he established the Shugei Shuchiin School where Buddhism and Confucianism were major subjects.

Master Kūkai wrote a number of works both on religious doctrines and literary, including *Benkenmitsu-nikyōron*, *Hizō-hōyaku*, *Jujushinron* (The Ten Stages of Religious Consciousness) , *Himitsu mandarakyo fuhoden*, *Sokushin-jōbutsu-gi*, *Unji-gi*, *Hannyashingyō-hiken*, *Bunkyohifuron* and *Shoryoshu* (Collected Works of Prose and Poetry of Kūkai) .

Nowadays, Chi'an, Xiapu is known as the landing place of Master Kūkai, and Fuzhou Kaiyuan Temple the first Buddhist temple Master Kūkai visited in

China. In the temple there are several memorials donated by the Japan Buddhist community, such as a stele indicating "the landing spot of Master Kūkai entering Tang China", a standing statue, a sitting statue, and a Dharmakaya stupa of Master Kūkai, and a tree of Sino-Japanese friendship. For the commemoration of Master Kūkai's stay at this temple, Fuzhou Kaiyuan Temple built the Memorial Hall of Master Kūkai. As the first temple Master Kūkai stayed in China and the home of Japanese Shingon Buddhism, Fuzhou Kaiyuan Temple is visited and worshiped by various social actors and Shingon monks from Japan every year.

日本天台宗寺门派宗祖

——圆珍大师

圆珍大师（814—891），俗姓和气，字远尘，日本赞岐国那珂郡人。圆珍是日本真言宗创始人空海大师的侄女佐伯氏之子，出家后投日本天台宗创始人最澄大师的弟子义真门下，年仅37岁便晋升为"传灯大法师"之位。

其后，圆珍入唐求法，在华六年，回国后被任命为日本天台宗第五代座主，圆寂后，赐号"智证大师"。圆珍入唐时，曾用汉文写有游唐日记《行历抄》，详细记录了他从福建福州连江登岸，至福州、温州、台州、越

州、长安的一路见闻，圆珍大师晚年的朋友、三善清行撰写了《天台宗延历寺座主圆珍传》，这些是我们今天了解圆珍大师的珍贵史料。

圆珍在华期间曾到福州在开元寺研习佛经 3 年。他师从住持存式法师学《妙法莲华经》《华严经》《俱舍论》，并向当时驻锡开元寺的中天竺三藏大师般若怛罗学习梵文与密教。在开元寺学习悉昙与密法的经历，对圆珍后来的求法与弘法活动产生了重大影响。

圆珍从小就气宇非凡，不同常人。15 岁时，他到日本天台宗的根本道场比叡山，投义真大师门下学习，得到义真大师赏识。义真是最澄大师的嗣法弟子，被日本天皇任命为第一代天台座主。

20 岁时，他正式出家，得度受戒，之后凭借过人的智慧和精进的修行，先后被朝廷授予为传灯满位、传灯法师位。

公元 847 年，后来成为日本第三代天台座主的圆仁，在入华九年后，终于学成回到日本。包括圆珍在内的比叡山僧众，瞻礼了圆仁带回的曼陀罗和密教经籍，均赞叹不已。之后，圆珍又在圆仁的指点下，学习大悲胎藏大法。第二年，圆珍年仅 37 岁就晋升传灯大法师位。这是极为难得的。

公元 853 年，圆珍在权臣藤原良房等人的支持下入唐。与之前日本入华高僧不同，圆珍不是跟随官方派遣的遣唐使，而是通过民间途径随商船入唐。圆珍所乘的商船，目的地是中国东南沿海的重要贸易港口福州。圆珍把入唐首刹选择在福州开元寺，有研究者认为，估计与空海曾经驻锡过此寺并予赞叹有关。

时年八月，圆珍一行八人，跟着新罗商人王超、唐朝商人李延孝等人，一同搭乘钦良晖的商船，由日本的九州岛扬帆入唐。据说当时风力很

大，仅五天时间，船就驶近琉球。

据记载，圆珍等人在船上，已经远远看到有番人持着长戈利矛，在岸边等待船靠岸，当时船家们相信琉球番人是食人者。船主钦良晖绝望地哭出来，认为必死无疑。危难之际，圆珍念诵不动明王，突然刮起了一阵东南风，将船吹送向西北，隔日抵达了福州连江县靠泊。

圆珍登岸后，被安排在福州开元寺等待地方当局的公验。圆珍入唐时，正值"会昌法难"结束不久。福州开元寺作为福州在此次法难中唯一幸存的寺院，高僧云集，规模在福州首屈一指，亦是当时全国十大寺之一。在福州开元寺期间，圆珍不仅师从寺僧存式法师学习，尤其天台宗教法，如学习了《妙法莲华经》等，还求得天台宗重要经疏《法华文句》十卷。在入唐首刹福州开元寺学习了天台教法和密法的圆珍，后来对日本天台密教（台密）的形成，贡献良多。

圆珍住开元寺期间，与空海交情甚厚的惠灌法师询问圆珍："五笔和尚"（即空海）还健在吗？圆珍答：认识大僧正空海法师，但已作古。惠灌法师闻讯拍胸流涕，悲叹说：不能再和空海切磋交流了。福州开元寺惠灌法师与空海、圆珍两位的交往，成为中日佛教交流的一段佳话。

据圆珍后来在《开元寺求得经疏目录》中记载，在福州开元寺期间，他共得到大小乘各类经论一百五十六卷，其中包括《不空羂索陀罗尼经》等密教典籍，更获般若怛罗大师亲赠"中天竺大那烂陀寺贝多叶梵字真言一夹""梵字无碍大悲心陀罗尼一夹"，以及法器带有指环的熟铜"五钴金刚杵"一枚。

圆珍大师后到浙江天台山国清寺，拟继续学习天台教义，但因"法

难"原因，高僧四散，寺院荒废，但他坚持居住。唐大中九年（855）至长安青龙寺，从法全受瑜伽密旨，受传阿阇黎位灌顶；又向大兴善寺智慧轮学胎藏、金刚两部秘法。后到洛阳祭拜金刚智大师之墓，并完成《大日经义释》的点校。最后，他又回到天台山。当初日本天台宗祖师最澄大师入唐时，曾在天台山禅林寺建造一院，以备后来学法的僧侣居住，院舍后来颓毁。圆珍大师在国清寺建起了"日本国大德僧院"，以便后世日本僧人来华交流，圆满了最澄大师的心愿。

唐大中十二年（858），圆珍大师携带经疏千余卷回国。是日本"入唐八大家"中，携回佛教经论最多的僧人。他依敕命住比睿山山王院，并屡次受请入宫讲经修法。第二年，他在三井建立园城寺，奏请为日本天台宗的别院。园城寺的藏经院因保存了大量圆珍大师从唐朝带回的经籍法宝，也被称为"唐院"。

864年，在仁寿殿设立大悲胎藏的灌顶坛，入坛者有天皇及大臣藤原良相等三十余人。866年，又在冷然院建立持念坛，专为宝祚长久进行祈祷。

868年，圆珍大师回国十年后，被推举为日本第五代天台座主，在职共二十四年。其门人有惟首、猷宪等，此后相继继任日本天台座主。

宽平三年（891）十月二十九日圆寂，年78岁。传世有《法华论记》《授决集》《大日经指归》等著作。延长五年（927）十二月，日本醍醐天皇追赐圆珍大师"智证大师"谥号。

日本天台宗分为最澄大师开创的根本大师流、圆仁大师开创的慈觉大师流、圆珍大师开创的智证大师流（即寺门派）。圆珍大师后来被尊为日

本天台宗寺门派的宗祖。

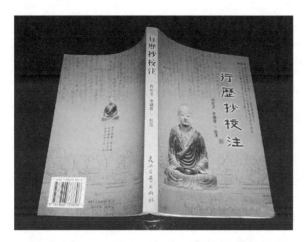

天台宗自最澄大师起，就成为中日两国间佛教及文化交流的重要纽带。自唐以降，日本天台宗佛教徒来华修学或参礼朝拜者，不绝如缕。

目前，福州开元寺有圆珍大师法身纪念塔一座。法身纪念塔安立于2007年，当时日本国会众议院议员、日本内阁府政务官冈下信子女士一行，前来参加安立仪式。塔由冈下信子携木村朝映、青山惠美共同捐造。

日本天台宗寺門派宗祖

——円珍大師

　　円珍大師（814—891）、俗姓は和気、字は遠塵、日本讃岐国那珂郡に誕生した。日本真言宗開祖の空海大師の姪佐伯氏の息子にあたる。出家後、日本天台宗開祖の最澄大師の弟子義真に師事し、37歳の若さで「伝灯大法師位」を授けられた。

　　その後、円珍は入唐し、六年間修学した。帰国して日本天台宗第五世座主に任命され、入滅後「智証大師」の諡号が贈られた。円珍は漢文で入唐旅行日録『行歴抄』を書き、福建省連江に上陸して、福州、温州、台州、越州、長安までたどり着く途中の見聞を詳しく記載した。円珍大師晩年の友、三善清行が撰述した『天台宗延歴寺座主円珍伝』などの資料が、現在我々が円珍大師を知る貴重な史料である。

　　円珍は留学中、福州開元寺で三年間仏経を学習していた。住職の存式法師に師事し、『妙法蓮華経』『華厳経』『倶舎論』を学び、当時開元寺に滞在中のインド中部出身の高僧三蔵大師般若怛羅に梵語（サンスクリット語）と密教を教わった。開元寺で梵字と密教を学習した経験は、円珍大師今後の求法と付法に重大な影響を与えた。

　　円珍大師は幼少期から凡人と違って気位が高く、15歳のとき、日本

天台宗根本道場の比叡山に登り、義真大師の門に入り、義真大師に高く評価された。義真は最澄大師の法統を受け継ぐ弟子であり、日本天皇に第一世天台座主に任じされた。

　20歳のとき、円珍は得度受戒した。その後、人一倍の智慧と精進した修行によって、朝廷から伝灯満位、伝灯法師位を授けられた。

　西暦847年、後に日本第三世天台座主になった円仁大師が、入唐九年後ようやく帰朝した。円珍大師を含め、比叡山の僧侶だちは、円仁大師が持ってきた曼荼羅と密教経籍を拝礼し、みんな驚嘆した。その後、円珍大師は円仁大師の指導の下、大悲胎蔵大法を学習した。翌年、円珍大師はわずか37歳の年で、伝灯大法師位を授けられた。

　西暦853年、円珍大師は藤原良房らの支援によって唐の国に入った。以前の高僧たちと違って、円珍大師は国によって派遣された遣唐使ではなく、民間のルートで商船に乗って入唐したのだ。円珍大師が乗った商船の目的地は、中国東南沿岸部の重要な貿易港福州である。研究者によると、円珍大師は入唐して最初に福州開元寺に訪れた理由は、空海大師がこの寺に滞在し寺を賞賛したことにあると言われている。

　同年8月、円珍大師一行八人は、新羅の商人王超、唐の商人李延孝らに就いて、欽良暉の商船に同乗して、日本の九州島から出帆入唐した。強風に会ったため、五日間だけで琉球に漂着したと言われた。

　記載によると、円珍大師らは船から遠く離れた海辺で鋭利な長兵を持った当地の人たちを見かけた。その時、琉球人は食人者と見られていた。船主の欽良暉は絶望的に号泣し、必ずに死ぬと思っていた。危機一

髪の際、円珍大師は不動明王を唱えて、忽然と南東風が吹いてきて、船
を北西方面に吹かせて、翌日福州連江県に安着した。

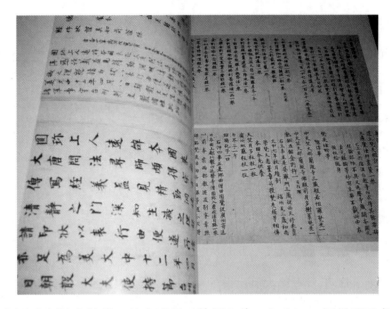

　　円珍大師は上陸後、地方当局の検証を待つために、福州開元寺に泊
まらせた。円珍大師が入唐した時は、ちょうど会昌法難（廃仏事件）が
終わったばかりの時期だった。福州開元寺は、会昌法難を経て福州で唯
一残った寺院として、高僧が集まり、福州屈指の規模を持ち、当時全国
十大寺院の一つに数えられていた。福州開元寺にいる間、円珍大師は存
式法師に師事し、特に『妙法蓮華経』などの天台宗教法を習得しただけ
でなく、天台宗重要な経書の『法華文句』を 10 巻求得した。入唐して
最初に滞在したお寺で天台教法と密教を習得した円珍大師は、後に日本
天台密教（台密）の形成に大きく貢献した。

　　円珍大師が福州開元寺に滞在した間、かつて空海大師と親交を結ん
だ恵潅法師は円珍に、「五筆和尚（空海のこと）は健在か否か」と尋ね

たという。入滅したと答えを受けた恵潅法師は、「また空海と切磋交流はできない」と涙を流して悲嘆した。福州開元寺の恵潅和尚法師と空海大師、円珍大師との親交は、中日仏教交流史でいい話を残した。

円珍大師は後に『開元寺求得経疏目録』を作成し、福州開元寺に滞在時、大乗、小乗各経論を合わせて165巻求得したことを記載した。その中に、『不空胃索陀羅尼経』などの密教典籍があり、般若怛羅大師から「中天竺大那爛陀寺貝多葉梵字真言一夾」、「梵字無碍大悲心陀羅尼一夾」、指輪を帯びた熟銅法具「五鈷金剛杵」を贈られた。

円珍大師は後に浙江省天台山国清寺に着き、続けて天台教義を習得しようとしたが、廃仏事件のせいで、高僧たちは四散し、寺院が廃棄された。それにもかかわらず、彼は依然として寺に居住していた。唐の大中9年（855）、円珍は長安の青龍寺に入り、法全のもとで瑜伽密旨の受法に励み、阿闍梨位潅頂を受けた。また、大興善寺智慧輪に胎蔵と金剛二つの秘法を勉学した。後に、洛陽に行き、金剛智大師のお墓に参詣し、『大日経義釈』の校勘を終えた。最後に、また天台山に戻った。当初、日本天台宗祖師の最澄大師が入唐時、求法する僧侶たちのために天台山禅林寺に一つの寺院を建てていたが、その寺院は毀損した。円珍大師は、後世日本の僧侶が訪中時、便利な施設を提供するために、国清寺で「日本国大徳僧院」を建て直し、最澄大師の願いを叶えた。

唐の大中12年（858）、円珍大師は千巻あまりの経書を持って帰朝した。「入唐八家」の中で、仏教経論を最も多く持参してきた僧侶である。勅命によって、比叡山の山王院に住し、何度も朝廷に入って講経修

法することを招聘された。翌年、三井で園城寺を修造し、日本天台宗の別院として申請登録した。園城寺の蔵経院は、円珍大師が唐から請来した経籍・法具を多数保存したため、「唐院」とも名づけられた。

864 年、仁寿殿に大悲胎蔵の潅頂壇を設け、天皇及び太政大臣藤原良相以下三十人あまりが参加した。866 年、冷然院に持念の壇を建て、長久に宝祚を祈り続けた。

868 年、円珍大師は帰朝十年後、日本天台宗第五世座主に推挙され、24 年間務めた。門下の惟首・猷憲らが相次ぎ日本天台座主に続任した。

寛平 3 年（891）10 月 29 日、円珍大師は入滅し、享年 78 歳。『法華論記』『授決集』『大日経指帰』などの著作を世に残した。延長 5 年（927）12 月、日本醍醐天皇より「智証大師」の諡号が贈られた。

日本天台宗は、最澄大師が開創した根本大師流、円仁大師が開創した慈覚大師流、円珍大師が開創した智証大師流（即ち寺門派）に分けている。円珍大師は後に日本天台宗寺門派の宗祖と仰がれた。

天台宗は最澄大師の時代より、中日両国仏教及び文化交流に重要の橋になった。唐の時代以降、日本天台宗の仏教信者は中国に来て、修学したり、拝礼したりして、訪問者は後を絶たない。

現在、福州開元寺に円珍大師法身記念塔が一座ある。法身記念塔は 2007 年に建立され、当時日本国会衆議院議員、内閣府政務官岡下信子一行が建立儀式に参列した。塔は、岡下信子をはじめ、木村朝映、青山恵美らによって共同寄付・建造された。

Founder of the Jimon School of Tendai Buddhism

—Master Enchin

Master Enchin (814—891) , who had the secular name Wake Enchin or Wake no Kimi, and the courtesy name Onjin, was born in Naka District, Sanuki Province, Japan. He was the child of a niece of Master Kūkai, who founded the Japanese Shingon Buddhism. After he took the tonsure, Enchin became a disciple of Gishin, who was a disciple of Master Saichō, the founder of Tendai Buddhism. At the age of 37, Enchin was granted the rank of "Great Master of Transmission of Light" .

Later, Enchin headed to Tang China to study Buddhist doctrines before he returned to Japan six years later and was appointed as the fifth zasu (head priest of the Tendai Sect) . After his death, Enchin was granted the posthumous title of Chishō Daishi. During his stay in China, Enchin wrote *Gyōrekishō* (Selection of Pilgrimage) , a travel diary in Chinese that recorded in detail his journey from Lianjiang, Fuzhou, Fujian Province, to Wenzhou, Taizhou, Yuezhou, and Chang'an. Enchin's friend Kiyotsura Miyoshi in his later years compiled *Tendaishu Enryakuji zasu Enchin den* (A Biography of Tendai Enryakuji Zasu

Enchin）. These are precious historical records for us today to learn about Master Enchin.

During his stay in China, Enchin studied Buddhist scriptures at Fuzhou Kaiyuan Temple for 3 years. He studied the *Lotus Sutra*, the *Avatamsaka Sutra*, and the *Abhidharmakośakārikā*（Verses on the Treasury of Abhidharma）from the abbot Cunshi, and learned Sanskrit and Esoteric Buddhism from the Indian Tripitaka Master Prajñātāra, who was then at Kaiyuan Temple. Enchin's experience of learning Siddhaṃ and Esoteric practices at Kaiyuan Temple had a major impact on his later efforts of seeking and propagating the Buddhist teachings.

Master Enchin had an extraordinary charisma since childhood. At the age of 15, he went to Mount Hiei, the fundamental dojo of the Tendai Sect, to learn from Master Gishin, who really appreciated Enchin's talents. As a disciple of Saichō, Gishin was appointed by the Japanese Emperor as the first zasu of the Tendai Sect.

At the age of 20, Enchin got ordained to become a Buddhist monk. Afterwards, he was awarded the Dentō Man-i（Senior Rank of Transmission of Light）and Dentō Hōshi-i（Rank of the Master of Transmission of Light）by virtue of his extraordinary wisdom and diligence.

In 847, Master Ennin, who later became the third zasu of the Tendai Sect, returned to Japan after nine years of study in China. The monks of Mount Hiei, Enchin included, paid tribute to the mandalas and Esoteric scriptures brought back by Master Ennin. Afterwards, Enchin learned the Womb Realm Mandala under the guidance of Master Ennin. In the following year, Enchin, at the age of 37, was promoted to Dentō Daihōshi-i (Rank of the Great Master of Transmission of Light) , which was an extremely rare case.

In 853, Master Enchin went to Tang China with the support of Fujiwara no Yoshifusa and others. Unlike his predecessors who entered China together with a mission dispatched by the Imperial Court of Japan to Tang, Enchin boarded a merchant ship for his travel. The merchant ship was destined for Fuzhou, an important trading port on the southeast coast of China. Master Enchin chose Fuzhou Kaiyuan Temple as the first destination upon his entry into China. Some researchers believe that he did so because Master Kūkai once resided at the temple and spoke highly of it.

In the eighth month of the same year, Master Enchin and his entourage, along with Silla businessman Wang Chao and Tang China businessman Li Yanxiao, boarded Qin Lianghui's merchant ship to set sail from Kyushu towards Tang China. It is said that the wind was so strong that it blew the ship to approach the Ryukyu Islands after five days.

According to historical records, Master Enchin and others on the ship saw from afar that there were people holding long spears waiting for the ship to dock. At that time, sailors generally believed Ryukyu islanders were man-eaters. The ship-owner Qin Lianghui cried out in despair, believing that they would all die for sure. At this juncture, Master Enchin chanted Acala's mantra. All of a sudden, a southeast wind started to blow the ship northwest until it arrived in Lianjiang County, Fuzhou, the next day.

After landing, Master Enchin was arranged to temporarily reside at Fuzhou Kaiyuan Temple to wait for the official inspection by the local authorities. Enchin's arrival was not long after the Great Anti-Buddhist Persecution initiated by Emperor Wuzong of Tang. As the only surviving temple in Fuzhou, Fuzhou Kaiyuan Temple were accommodating many eminent monks at that time, and being the largest temple in Fuzhou. It also ranked among the top ten temples in the country. During his stay at Fuzhou Kaiyuan Temple, Enchin not only learned Tiantai Buddhist scriptures, such as the *Lotus Sutra*, from Master Cunshi, but also was granted ten volumes of the *Words and Phrases of the Lotus Sutra*. His study of Tiantai Buddhist doctrines and Esoteric Buddhism at Fuzhou Kaiyuan Temple contributed significantly to the formation of the Tendai Buddhism in Japan.

When Master Enchin was living at the Kaiyuan Temple, Master Huiguan, who had a close relationship with Master Kūkai, asked Enchin: "Is the Buddhist Monk Master of Five Chinese Calligraphic Styles (that is, Master Kūkai) still alive?" Enchin replied: "I knew Kūkai, the Grand Master, but he has passed away." Hearing the news, Master Huiguan patted his chest, lamenting: "What a pity that I cannot communicate with Kūkai anymore!" The friendship between Master Huiguan of Fuzhou Kaiyuan Temple and the two Japanese Buddhist Masters of Kūkai and Enchin exemplifies the long-standing friendly exchanges between China and Japan in the Buddhist realm.

According to *A Memorial Presenting a List of Newly Imported Sutras from Kaiyuan Temple* by Master Enchin, during his stay at Fuzhou Kaiyuan Temple, Enchin received a total of 156 volumes of Mahayana and Hinayana sutras, including the *AmoghapāśahṛVday Sutra*. He was also granted by Master Prajñātāra "a piece of Sanskrit words on pattra from Nalanda" , "a piece of Sanskrit Mahā Karuṇā–citta Dhāranī" , and a refined copper–made "five–pronged vajra pestle" with rings affiliated.

Later, Master Enchin went to Guoqing Temple on Mount Tiantai, Zhejiang Province, planning to study Tiantai Buddhist doctrines. However, due to the Great Anti–Buddhist Persecution, the monks at Guoqing Temple had all fled, leaving the temple deserted. Nevertheless, Master Enchin decided to stay. In the ninth year of the Dazhong era (855) of the Tang dynasty, Enchin headed to Qinglong Temple in Chang'an, where he learned Tantra Yoga, and received the abhisheka of Esoteric Buddhism from the Ācārya Faquan. At Daxingshan Temple, he received initiations into the Womb Realm Mandala and the Diamond Realm Mandala under the Buddhist monk Zhihuilun. Then, in Luoyang, he worshiped at the tomb of Master Vajrabodhi, and completed the review of *Commentary to the Mahāvairocana Sutra*. Finally, he returned to Mount Tiantai. When Master Saichō came to China, he built a courtyard in Chanlin Temple on Mount Tiantai for the residence of Japanese monks who later sought Buddhist teachings. However, the courtyard was later turned into ruins. Following Master Saichō's footsteps, Enchin established a courtyard in Guoqing Temple to serve as a place to accommodate later generations of Japanese monks who came to China for exchanges.

In the twelfth year of the Dazhong era（858）of the Tang dynasty, Master Enchin returned to Japan with more than a thousand volumes of Buddhist scriptures. Among the eight Japanese Buddhist monks who came to China during the Tang dynasty, he was the one who brought back the largest number of Buddhist works. Upon his return, Master Enchin was ordered by the Japanese Emperor to live in the Sannoin on Mount Hiei, and was repeatedly invited to the imperial palace to preach Buddhist doctrines. In the following years, Enchin established Onjōji Temple（now Mii–dera）, and presented a memorial to the Japanese Emperor, requesting to make it a separate venue for Tendai Buddhism. Onjōji Temple preserved a large number of Buddhist scriptures and treasures brought back by Master Enchin from the Tang China. Therefore, it is also known as the Tōin（Tang Hall）.

In 864, a ritual altar for the Womb Realm Mandala was set up in the Jijuden Hall, where over 30 people, including the Japanese Emperor and Fujiwara no Yoshimi underwent the abhisheka. In 866, a prayer altar was established in the Reizeiin（an imperial palace for the emperor who abdicated the throne during the Heian period）to pray for the long–standing reign of the throne.

In 868, ten years after he returned to Japan, Master Enchin was elected as the fifth zasu of the Tendai Sect and served in the position for a total of 24 years. His disciples included Yuishu, Yūken, who served successively as the zasus of the Tendai Sect.

On the twenty–ninth day of the tenth month of the third year of the Kanpyō era（891）, Master Enchin passed away. His works that have been passed to later generations include *Hokke ron ki*（Commentary on the Treatise on the Lotus Sūtra）, *Juketsu shu*（Collection of Orally Transmitted Teachings）, and *Dainichikyō-shiiki*（The Essentials of the the Mahāvairocana Sutra）. In the twelfth month of the fifth year of the Enchō era（927）, Japanese Emperor Daigo granted Enchin the posthumous title of Chishō Daishi.

Japanese Tendai Buddhism is divided into three major schools, represented, respectively, by Saichō, Ennin and Enchin. Master Enchin was later revered as the founder of the Jimon school of Tendai Buddhism.

Tendai Buddhism has been an important bridge for the Buddhist and cultural exchanges between China and Japan since Master Saichō. Since the Tang dynasty, numerous Buddhists of the Tendai Sect came to China on a study tour or pilgrimage.

At present, there is a memorial stupa representing Master Enchin's Dharmakaya in Fuzhou Kaiyuan Temple. Built in 2007, the stupa was donated jointly by Nobuko Okashita, Tomoe Kimura, and Emi Aoyama. Ms. Nobuko Okashita, a member of the House of Representatives of Japan and the Administrative Officer of the Cabinet Office, came for its debut.

日本遣唐大使

——藤原葛野麻吕

藤原葛野麻吕（755—818），在公元 804 年以遣唐大使身份，率领最澄、空海、橘逸势等日后日本的名僧、名人，分乘四艘船赴唐。其乘坐的第一艘船被暴风吹到福州长溪（今福建霞浦），几经交涉，被安置驻留于福州开元寺。同年到达长安谒见唐德宗皇帝。805 年归国，官升至从三位，列名公卿。

藤原葛野麻吕是日本贵族藤原北家、大纳言藤原小黑麻吕的长子。因妹妹藤原上子为桓武天皇后宫而深受重用。

785 年叙从五位下，历任摄津次官、陆奥介、少纳言、右少辨。之后任平安京的造宫使。

794 年任皇太子安殿亲王（后来的平城天皇）的春宫大夫。任正五位下左少辨。

795 年升从四位下，任左中辨。796 年升从四位上。797 年任右大辨。

唐代是中日两国频繁友好往来的时代。在这一时期，日本多次向唐朝派遣遣唐使，大规模地吸收唐朝先进的文化。据研究史料，从公元 630 年到 894 年，200 多年间，日本共向唐朝派出遣唐使 19 次，但成功抵达者只有 8 次，其余 11 次均失败。

据《日本后纪》等史书记载，公元 801 年，藤原葛野麻吕被任命为遣唐大使，兼越前守。临出发前，在大殿之上举行饯行宴会，都依照汉朝时的礼仪。桓武天皇在御床之下赐酒，并作和歌慰劳他。藤原葛野麻吕对天皇的恩宠十分感动，落下了眼泪。桓武天皇赐给藤原葛野麻吕御被三领、御衣一袭、黄金二百两。在辞行前的会面中，藤原葛野麻吕又接受了天皇赐予的节刀。803 年他率队出发，但因风暴毁舶，渡海失败，准备一年以后，重新启航。

公元 804 年（日本延历二十三年，唐朝贞元二十年），进爵为从四位上。在大殿上举行饯行宴会的时候，天皇下令奏乐，并赐给藤原葛野麻吕宝琴一张。

为了确保安全，船队经过近两个月的实习和准备，于七月初六正式出发。由大使藤原葛野麻吕和副使石川道益率领，分乘四船前往唐朝。

据《弘法大师空海传》记载，空海所乘的第一艘船上共有23个人，包括大使藤原葛野麻吕及学者、僧侣等。

据后来藤原葛野麻吕给恒武天皇的陈奏，其所乘第一船"去年七月六日发从肥前国松浦郡田浦"，但很快与另外3艘船失去联系，"出入死生之间，掣曳波涛之上，都卅四个日。八月十日到福州长溪县赤岸镇已南海口"。可见藤原葛野麻吕一行在海上漂泊长达34天之久，才到达长溪赤岸。

当年，日本遣唐使赴中国有南北两条规定的路线。北边的一条，是绕过新罗（今韩国南部），渡过黄海，在山东靠岸，然后顺陆路直抵长安。南边的一条，是经日本九州岛，渡过东海，在江苏一带登岸。登陆后，都有长安指派的专人迎接。

因为船队在途中遭遇暴风雨，藤原葛野麻吕率领的第一艘船漂泊到福州长溪，最澄乘坐的第二艘船漂泊到明州（今宁波），第三艘船被风刮回日本九州，第四艘船则下落不明。

藤原葛野麻吕一行到了赤岸，非但没人迎接，反而不准登陆。因为这里不是朝廷原先设定的外国人士登陆点。

空海大师《御遗告》一书中，对于遣唐使船停靠福州长溪赤岸的情况有翔实的描写："延历二十三年五月十二日入唐……彼海路间三千里。先例至于扬、苏州，无质。介此度船增七百里，到衡州多碍。此间，大使越前国太守、正三位藤原朝臣贺能（贺能是葛野麻吕的中国名字），自作手书呈衡州司。州司批看即以此文弃了。如此两三度。虽然封船追人，居湿沙上。此时，大使述云，切愁之今也，抑大德（空海）笔主，使呈书云

云。兹吾作书样替大使呈彼州长。批览含笑，开船加问。即奏长安，经三十九日，给州府力使四人，且给资粮。州长好问，作借屋十三间与住。经五十八日，给存问敕使等。彼仪式，无极。览此主客各各，流泪。次给后迎客使。给大使以七珍之鞍，次次使等皆给妆鞍。长安入京仪式，不可尽说。"（这是空海大师回国30多年后的回忆录。衡州系"福州"笔误）

据上文可知，藤原葛野麻吕一行到赤岸后，再三上书给当时的地方官，但是没有结果，船被封，人不能上岸，藤原葛野麻吕一筹莫展，于是便请精通汉文的留学生空海代笔。空海即书一文，言辞恳切地将奉国命入唐、漂流至此的经过诉说一番，呈送给当时的福建观察使兼福州刺史阎济美。阎济美看到此书后，大加赞赏，对藤原葛野麻吕一行予以信任，一边上报长安，一边安排食物和使役人等，并要求当时安置外国僧侣的官方驿所福州芝山开元寺，紧急安排房屋十三间供他们居住。

延历二十三年（804）十一月三日，藤原葛野麻吕率领空海等人离开福州，踏上去长安的路程。

十一月二十四日，藤原葛野麻吕在长安献上贡物，唐德宗欣然接纳。

十一月二十五日，唐德宗在宣化殿接见了藤原葛野麻吕一行。

第二年（805）二月十一日，藤原葛野麻吕等完成了出使任务，允准回归日本。空海和另一名留学生橘逸势两人则敕准在长安留学。

藤原葛野麻吕回国后，因出使唐朝的功劳，被进封为从三位，列名公卿。

大同元年（806），出任参议、兼任式部卿，又担任东海道观察使，不久担任中纳言，进封正三位，兼任皇太弟傅。

大同五年（810），发生藤原药子政变。政变失败后，嵯峨天皇认为藤原葛野麻吕与藤原药子有亲戚关系，想要定他的重罪。由于多入鹿向天皇证明藤原葛野麻吕的无辜，才没有治他的罪。不久迁任民部卿。

弘仁九年（818）十一月十日，藤原葛野麻吕去世，享年64岁。官位是正三位，中纳言。

承和八年（834），日仁明天皇承和元年正月，藤原葛野麻吕的儿子藤原常嗣也被任命为遣唐大使。

日本遣唐大使

——藤原葛野麻呂

藤原葛野麻呂（755—818）が西暦804年に遣唐大使として、後に日本の名僧、名人になった最澄、空海、橘逸勢らを率いて、四隻の船に乗って唐の国に渡航した。彼が乗った第一隻の船は暴風雨に会って、福州長渓（現在福建の霞浦）に漂着した。何度もの交渉を経た結果、福州開元寺に滞留されることになった。同年、長安に入り、唐の徳宗皇帝への謁見を果たした。805年帰国し、官位は従三位にまで昇格され、公卿に列した。

藤原葛野麻呂は、日本貴族の藤原北家、大納言藤原小黒麻呂の長男である。妹の藤原上子が桓武天皇の後宮に入ったために重んじられる。

785年、従五位下に叙され、摂津次官、陸奥介、少納言、右少弁に歴任した。その後、平安京の造宮使に任ぜられた。

794年、皇太子・安殿親王（後の平城天皇）の春宮大夫に務め、正五位下・左少弁に叙任された。

795年、従四位下・左中弁に任ぜられた。797年、右大弁に叙任された。

唐の時代、中日両国の友好交流は盛んに行われていた。この時期

に、日本から遣唐使は中国に頻繁に派遣され、唐の進んだ文化を大規模で受容した。研究史料により、630 年から 894 年までの 200 年あまりにわたって、日本から中国に 19 回の遣唐使が任命されたが、渡航に成功したのは 8 回だけで、11 回はみんな失敗に終わった。

　　『日本後記』などの史書の記載により、西暦 801 年、藤原葛野麻呂は遣唐大使に任命され、越前守を兼任した。出発前、大殿で漢代の儀礼によって送別会を行った。桓武天皇は御床のもとで酒を賜り、俳句を歌って藤原葛野麻呂を激励した。藤原葛野麻呂は天皇の恩寵に感動し、涙を流した。桓武天皇より御被三件、御衣一件、黄金二百両を授けられた。お別れの面会で、また恩賜の節刀を授けられた。803 年、藤原葛野麻呂は隊を率いて出発したが、暴風雨を受けて遣唐使船が破損して、航海は取りやめになった。一年間の準備を経て、再度出航しようとした。

　　西暦 804 年（日本延暦 23 年、唐の貞元 20 年）、藤原葛野麻呂は従四位上に昇格した。大殿で送別会を行った時、天皇は奏楽を命令し、宝琴を 1 面授けた。

　　安全を確保するため、船隊は二ヶ月近くの操練と準備を繰り返して、7 月 6 日に正式に出発した。藤原葛野麻呂は遣唐大使として、石川道益は副使として、四隻の船に分けて唐の国へと向かった。

　　『弘法大師空海伝』の記載によって、空海が乗った第一船では、大使の藤原葛野麻呂や学者、僧侶など 23 人が同乗した。

　　後に、藤原葛野麻呂が桓武天皇に上奏したように、彼が乗った第一船は、「去年七月六日肥前国松浦郡田浦より発し、四船海に入る」。しか

し、間もなくほかの三船と連絡を断ち、「死生の間に出入し、波濤の上を掣曳せらるること、都て卅四箇日。八月十日、福州長渓縣赤岸鎮巳南の海口に到る。」これより、藤原葛野麻呂一行は34日間も海で漂泊して、ようやく長渓赤岸に到着したことを伺える。

　その時、日本遣唐使が中国に渡航する路線は二つある。北の路線は、新羅（現在韓国南部）を回って、黄海を渡って山東に上陸し、陸路を利用して長安に向かう。南の路線は、日本九州島を経由して、中国東海を渡って、江蘇あたりに上陸する。どちらも長安からの専門使者が港で出迎えしている。

　船隊は途中で暴風雨に会ったことから、藤原葛野麻呂が率いた第一船は福州長渓に漂着した。最澄が乗った第二船は明州（現在の寧波市）に漂着した。第三船は風に日本九州に吹き返された。第四船は行方不明になった。

　　藤原葛野麻呂一行は赤岸に到着したら、出迎えの人がいないだけで
なく、上陸さえ許可されていなかった。ここは朝廷が設置した外国人氏
を受ける上陸地ではないためである。

　　空海大師が書いた『御遺告』の中で、遣唐使船が福州長渓に停留し
たことについて詳しく記載している。「延暦23年5月12日入唐……唐
との海路の距離は三千里である。以前ならば、揚州、蘇州に到着するに
は何の問題もなかった。ところが、今回、私の乗った船は、途中で様々
な難関に会って、七百里も増して衡州に漂着した。その間、遣唐大使
の越前国の太守・正三位藤原朝臣賀能（賀能は葛野麻呂の中国語の名
前）は、自ら親書を作って衡州の長官に送った。州の長官は、その文書
を見ただけで捨ててしまった。二、三回も文書を送ることを繰り返し
ていた。しかしながら、船は閉じてしまい、一行を追いやって湿った
砂辺に居らせた。この時、大使の藤原賀能が、『今は極めて憂うべき時
だ。達筆の貴方（空海）が私に代わって文書を差し出してください』な
どと言った。そこで私は、文書を書いて、大使に代わって州の長官に提
出した。長官は文書を見て笑みを浮かべ、船を開き、事情の聴取などを
した。すぐに長安に申し伝えるのに三十九日間が過ぎたら、州の役所か
ら世話係四人を派遣し、あわせて物資や食糧を支給してくれた。州の長
官は親切に尋ねてきて、宿舎として家屋十三棟を貸して一行を住まわせ
た。五十八日間が過ぎると、遣唐使一行の安否を問う勅使などが来てく
れた。その礼儀作法は極まりないものであった。これを見る唐の人もう
ちの人も、みなそれぞれ涙を流した。その後、客を迎えるための使者で

ある迎客使が来てくれた。大使は七宝で飾られた鞍をいただき、同行の次々の遣唐使の者たちにはみんな飾った鞍が贈られた。長安に入る儀式は、言い表せないほど盛大であった。」（これは空海大師が帰朝して30年後書いた回顧録であり、「衡州」は「福州」の誤記とされる。）

前文からよれば、藤原葛野麻呂一行は赤岸に到着したら、何度も当時の地方役人に文書を提出したが、返事をもらっていないまま、船は封じれて、人も上陸できないことがわかった。藤原葛野麻呂は途方に暮れた時に、中国語に精通した空海に代筆させた。空海は即時に文書を書き、朝廷の指示に従って入唐し、この地まで漂着した経緯を説明し、福州観察使兼福州刺史の閻済美宛に提出した。閻済美はその手紙を見たら、書の素晴らしさに感銘を受け、藤原葛野麻呂一行を信用し、長安に報告する一方、食糧と使役者を手配して、外国人僧侶を応接する公式宿駅の福州芝山開元寺に、13棟家屋を緊急手配することを要請し、一行を宿泊させた。

延暦23年（804）11月3日、藤原葛野麻呂は空海らを率いて福州を出て、長安に向けて旅立った。

11月24日、藤原葛野麻呂は長安で献上品を納め、唐の徳宗皇帝が喜んで引き受けた。

11月25日、唐の徳宗皇帝が宣化殿で藤原葛野麻呂一行を接待した。

翌年（805）2月21日、藤原葛野麻呂らは遣唐使の任務を達成し、帰国が許可された。空海及びもう一人の留学生橘逸勢は長安で留学することが勅許された。

　　藤原葛野麻呂は帰国後、遣唐大使の功労により、従三位に昇叙され公卿に列した。

　　大同元年（806）、参議に昇進し、式部卿を兼ねた。東海道観察使の後に中納言に任ぜられ、正三位に叙任されて、皇太弟傅を兼任した。

　　大同5年（810）、藤原薬子の変が発生した。変後の処置では藤原薬子と縁戚関係であった事から嵯峨天皇より重罪とされるが、多入鹿が天皇に藤原葛野麻呂の無実を証明したため、処罰を逃れた。しばらくしたら、民部卿に転任した。

　　弘仁9年（818）11月10日、藤原葛野麻呂は死去し、享年64歳である。最終官位は正三位中納言である。

　　承和8年（834）、仁明天皇承和元年正月、藤原葛野麻呂の息子藤原常嗣も遣唐大使に任命された。

Japanese Envoy to Tang China

—Fujiwara no Kadanomaro

In 804, Fujiwara no Kadanomaro (755—818) , as a Japanese envoy dispatched to Tang China, led four ships to Tang China, accompanied by Saichō, Kūkai, and Tachibana no Hayanari, among others who would later become prominent Japanese monks and celebrities. The first ship Fujiwara no Kadanomaro boarded was blown off course to Changxi, Fuzhou (now Xiapu, Fujian Province) by storm. After several negotiations, they were accommodated in Fuzhou Kaiyuan Temple. In the same year, Fujiwara no Kadanomaro arrived in Chang'an, the capital of Tang China, to meet the Chinese Emperor Dezong of Tang dynasty. After returning to Japan in 805, he was promoted to the Junior Third Rank as a Kugyō (a collective term for the very few most powerful men attached to the court of the Emperor of Japan in pre-Meiji eras) .

Fujiwara no Kadanomaro was the eldest son of the Dainagon (counselor of the first rank in the Imperial Court of Japan) Fujiwara no Oguromaro of the noble Fujiwara Hokke clan. He was appointed major positions as his sister Fujiwara no Joshi was a concubine of Emperor Kanmu.

In 785, Fujiwara no Kadanomaro was bestowed the court rank of Jugoige

（Junior Fifth Rank, Lower Grade）. He served successively as Vice Governor of Settsu Province, Vice Governor of Mutsu Province, Shōnagon（counselor of the third rank in the Imperial Court of Japan）, and Ushoben（Minor Controller of the Right）. Later, he was appointed as the palace building emissary of Heian-kyō（now Kyoto）.

In 794, he was appointed as Master of the Crown Prince's Quarters for the Crown Prince Ate（later Emperor Heizei）. He served as Sashoben（Minor Controller of the Left）, Senior Fifth Rank, Lower Grade.

In 795, he was appointed as Sachuben（Middle Controller of the Left）, Junior Fourth Rank, Lower Grade. In 797, he was appointed as Udaiben（Major Controller of the Right）. In 804, he was promoted to Junior Fourth Rank, Upper Grade.

China's Tang dynasty（618—907）saw frequent friendly exchanges between China and Japan. During this period, Japan dispatched missions to China on multiple occasions to learn from the advanced culture of the Tang dynasty. According to historical records, from 630 to 894, Japan sent missions to Tang China 19 times, though with 8 successes only.

According to *Nihon Koki* and other historical books, in 801, Fujiwara no Kadanomaro was appointed as the Japanese Envoy to Tang China and also the Governor of Echizen Province. Before departing, a banquet was held in the imperial palace in accordance with the etiquette of the Han dynasty（202 BC–220 AD）of China. Japanese Emperor Kanmu bestowed wine upon him and composed a waka (a type of poetry in classical Japanese literature) as a way to express his best wishes for the voyage. Deeply moved by the Emperor's favor, Fujiwara no Kadanomaro shed tears. Emperor Kanmu also bestowed upon him three quilts, one piece of clothing, and two hundred taels of gold. In his meeting with the Emperor before departure, Fujiwara no Kadanomaro received a ceremonial sword settō from the Emperor. In 803, the fleet set sail. However, severe storms damaged the ships and forced a return to Japan. After one year of preparation, the mission was sent out again.

In 804 (the twenty–third year of the Enryaku era, or the twentieth year of the Zhenyuan era) , Fujiwara no Kadanomaro was promoted to Jushiijo (Junior Fourth Rank, Upper Grade) . When holding a farewell banquet in the imperial palace, the Emperor gave orders to play music and bestowed a precious guqin upon Fujiwara no Kadanomaro.

To ensure safety, the fleet departed on the sixth day of the seventh month of the lunar calendar after nearly two months of drill and preparation. Led by the Envoy Fujiwara no Kadanomaro and the vice-secretary Ishikawa no Michimasu, the fleet, consisting of four ships, headed to Tang China.

According to *Biography of Kōbō-Daishi Kūkai*, there were a total of 23 people on the first ship that Kūkai boarded, including the Envoy Fujiwara no Kadanomaro, and some scholars and monks.

According to a memorial presented by Fujiwara no Kadanomaro later to the Japanese Emperor Kanmu, "the first ship set off from Tanoura, Matsuura District, Hizen Province on the sixth day of the seventh month in the last year, but soon lost contact with the other three ships". "The ship encountered storms, which put us on the brink of life and death for 34 days. On the tenth day of the eighth month, the ship eventually arrived at Chi'an Town, Changxi County, Fuzhou." This indicates that it took 34 days before the ship reached Chi'an Town.

At that time, there were two prescribed routes for Japan to send missions to Tang China, one on the north and the other on the south. The one on the north was to bypass Silla (now the southern and central parts of the Korean Peninsula), cross the Yellow Sea, land in Shandong Province, and then go straight to Chang'an by road. The one on the south was to cross the East China Sea via Kyushu, Japan, and land in Jiangsu Province. Generally, after their landing, they would be greeted by designated persons appointed by the

Government of Tang China.

Due to storms at sea, the first ship led by Fujiwara no Kadanomaro reached Changxi, Fuzhou; the second ship led by Saichō reached Mingzhou（now Ningbo）; and the third ship was forced to return to Kyushu, Japan; while the fourth ship went missing.

Fujiwara no Kadanomaro and his party arrived at Chi'an Town, just to find no one there greeting them, and they were initially opposed to make landfall, because it was not an official landing place for foreigners designated by the Imperial Court of Tang China.

In his book *Goyuigo*, Master Kūkai described in detail how the mission ship anchored at Chi'an Town, Changxi County, Fuzhou, "The ship entered Tang's territory on the twelfth day of the fifth month in the twenty-third year of Enryaku era... By then, we had traveled three thousand li（traditional Chinese unit of distance）across the sea. There were predecessors who arrived at Yangzhou and Suzhou without any disturbances. However, this time, our ship sailed seven hundred li more until we arrived at Hengzhou, with adversities along the way. At the time, the Envoy and Governor of Echizen Province Fujiwara no Kadanomaro, wrote a letter by himself to the Hengzhou Government. The Hengzhou governor threw it aside upon viewing it. This happened twice or three times. Prohibited from coming ashore, the ship was forced to drift on wet sand. At this time, the Envoy told me that he didn't know what to do, and requested that I write a letter to the governor as the last resort.

Therefore, I did it as requested. After reading my letter, the governor was really impressed, deciding to allow us to come onshore. The governor also reported to the central government, which took thirty-nine days. Four servants, as well as food, were bestowed by the local government. The governor was also very kind to lend thirteen rooms for us to live in. After fifty-eight days, a royal messenger was sent to express regards and concern for us. The ritual was so heartwarming that both the hosts and the guests burst into tears. The next day, welcoming envoys arrived. The Japanese Envoy was bestowed the Saddle of Seven Treasures, and the Vice-Secretary clothes and saddles. The ceremony held in Chang'an to welcome us was even more grand. I cannot mention all the details here." (The above is excerpted from the memoir of Master Kūkai 30 years after he returned to Japan. Hengzhou should be a typo for "Fuzhou" .)

According to the records above, when Fujiwara no Kadanomaro and his party arrived in Chi'an, they repeatedly appealed to the local official to go onshore, but were refused. Their ship was prohibited from anchoring and they were not allowed to go ashore. Stranded at nowhere, Fujiwara no Kadanomaro asked Kūkai, who was proficient in Chinese because he used to be a student studying in China, to write a letter. In the letter, Kūkai described in detail how Fujiwara no Kadanomaro and his party were sent as a mission to Tang China by the Japanese Emperor, and arrived at the place due to storms. The letter was presented to the then Fujian Observer and Fuzhou Governor Yan Jimei. Greatly impressed by the letter, Yan decided to trust what Fujiwara no Kadanomaro said.

While reporting to the central government, he arranged food and servants for the mission and requested Fuzhou Kaiyuan Temple, the official posthouse for foreign monks at that time, to vacate thirteen rooms to accommodate them.

On the third day of the eleventh month of the twenty–third year of the Enryaku era (804) , Fujiwara no Kadanomaro and his party left Fuzhou for Chang'an.

On the twenty–fourth day of the eleventh month, Fujiwara no Kadanomaro presented tributes to Emperor Dezong of the Tang dynasty in Chang'an.

On the twenty–fifth day of the eleventh month, Emperor Dezong met Fujiwara no Kadanomaro and his party in the Xuanhua Hall.

On the eleventh day of the second month of the next year (805) , Fujiwara no Kadanomaro and his party were allowed to return to Japan after completing their mission. Kūkai and the other Japanese student, Tachibana no Hayanari, were allowed to continue studying in Chang'an.

After returning to Japan, Fujiwara no Kadanomaro was promoted to Junior Third Rank because of his successful mission to Tang China.

In the first year of the Daido era (806) , he was appointed as Sangi (Associate Counselor) and Shikibu–kyō (Minister of Ceremonial Affairs) , as well as Observer of the Tōkaidō. Soon he was appointed as Chūnagon (Middle Counselor) , and promoted to Senior Third Rank. In the meantime, he also served as the master of the Emperor's younger brother.

In the fifth year of the Daido era (810) under Emperor Saga's reign, the

Kusuko Incident occurred, where the retired Emperor Heizei and his lover Fujiwara no Kusuko staged a coup against the incumbent Emperor Saga. When the coup was appeased, Emperor Saga intended to convict Fujiwara no Kadanomaro of felony due to his relationship with Fujiwara no Kusuko. Fujiwara no Kadanomaro was not convicted eventually, thanks to the official Oo no Iruka's effort to prove his innocence to the Emperor. Before long, he was appointed as Minbu-kyō (Minister of Popular Affairs) .

On the tenth day of the eleventh month of the ninth year of the Kōnin era (818) , Fujiwara no Kadanomaro died at the age of 64. He was then serving as Chūnagon, Senior Third Rank.

In the first month of the first year of the Jōwa era (834) , his son Fujiwara no Tsunetsugu was also appointed as the official envoy to Tang China.

日本"书道三笔"之一

——橘逸势

橘逸势（782—842），日本平安时代著名书法家，与空海、嵯峨天皇被共称日本"书道三笔"。橘逸势出身名门，其曾祖父橘诸兄是日本奈良时代的正一位左大臣，其祖父为橘奈良麻吕，其父橘入居。橘入居有两个女儿，是恒武天皇（781—806 年在位）称为女御的后宫。橘逸势在家中排行第三。

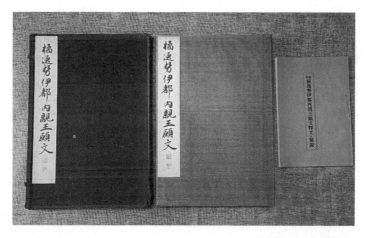

延历二十三年（804），20 多岁的橘逸势与空海等一同随遣唐使到中国留学，曾住于福州开元寺。在中国期间，除了学习汉语，他还学习了古琴与书法。他潜心研究中国书法大家李北海以及大文豪柳宗元的学问。他仰慕柳宗元的诗文，曾登门求教。

在日本"书道三笔"中，橘逸势是最具有唐人书风的。其深厚的汉学修养和风流倜傥的性格，与唐代文人雅士毫无二致。他非凡的才能令唐人惊叹，被亲切地称为"橘秀才"。

日本平城天皇大同元年（806）八月，橘逸势又与空海大师一道搭乘遣唐使判官高阶远成的船返回日本。

遣唐留学生回国后，都由日本朝廷按其所学，安排在政界，或教育、医药、刑律、艺术等不同部门工作。但橘逸势回国后，仕途并不顺利，可能是他的性格使然。《续日本后纪》对他性格的评价是"放诞，不拘细节"。

到承和七年（840），他仅被任命为官职较小的但马权守。

然而，较低的社会地位并没有影响他成为声名卓著的书法家。818年，日本嵯峨天皇亲自题写了大内里东面三门的匾额，名僧空海题写了南面三门的匾额，而北面三门的匾额是由橘逸势题写的。

空海大师当时已经是日本佛教真言宗的开山祖师，社会地位极高。地位较低的橘逸势与嵯峨天皇、空海大师所题匾额能够并列排放，可见橘逸势的书法在当时的日本深受推崇。

然而，承和九年（842），嵯峨天皇死后第二日，他卷入了围绕皇位继承展开的政治斗争，后以谋反罪被流放到伊豆半岛。

8月13日，在流放遣送的途中，病入膏肓的他，病死在远江国的板筑客栈里。

据说他的独生女在他流配伊始，便日夜兼程地跟随其后。父亲死后，她削发为尼，在墓地前建庵守坟。有一种说法是，她将父亲的遗体背回了

京城。总之，孝女妙沙尼的事迹广为流传，感动了很多人，终于在嘉祥三年（850），橘逸势得以归葬故里。

仁寿三年（853），文德天皇为他恢复了名誉和橘氏本姓，并追赠从四位下的品位。

橘逸势如今留存于世、可确信无疑的书法真迹，只有《伊都内亲王愿文》，这篇作品内容为写给伊都亲王的愿文。书风令人刮目，其与李北海相似但自成一家，文字点画形态流露出对二王的继承，但整幅作品表现的意趣更接近唐人。浓重的笔触和开阔的气势，是对带有一定婉约色彩的二王书风的革新。

日本「書道三筆」の一人

——橘逸勢

　橘逸勢（782—842）、日本平安時代有名な書家、空海、嵯峨天皇と共に日本「書道三筆」と呼ばれている。貴族の出身、曽祖父の橘諸兄は日本奈良時代初期の正一位左大臣、祖父は橘奈良麻呂、父は橘入居。橘入居の娘二人は桓武天皇（在位781—806年）の後宮の女御である。橘逸勢は末子である。

　延暦23年（804）、20代の橘逸勢は空海大師らと共に遣唐使として唐に渡り、空海大師と同じく福州開元寺に滞在したことがある。在唐中、中国語だけでなく、琴と書も習得した。中国書家李北海や大文豪柳宗元の学問を専念して勉強した。柳宗元の詩文に憧れて、訪ねて教わったこともあるといわれている。

　日本「書道三筆」の中で、橘逸勢は最も唐の書風を備えた一人である。深い漢学の教養と放胆で大らかな性格は唐の時代の文人と全く同じである。彼が優れた才能を持つことから、唐の官人たちは「橘秀才」と呼んで驚嘆した。

　日本平城天皇大同元年（806）8月、橘逸勢は空海大師と一緒に遣唐使判官高階遠成の船に乗って日本に戻った。

　遣唐留学生は帰国後、日本朝廷がそれぞれの学識によって、政界や教育、医薬、刑法、芸術など異なった部署に配属される。しかし、橘逸勢は帰国したら、性格のせいか、官吏の道はうまく行っていない。『続日本後紀』によって、彼の性格は放胆で、細かいことに拘らなかったという。

　承和7年（840）、橘逸勢は比較的に低い官職の但馬権守に任命された。

　しかしながら、比較的に低い社会地位に居ながらも、橘逸勢は能書家として名をはせた。818年、嵯峨天皇は大内裏東の三門の門額を自筆し、南の三門を空海に書かせ、北の三門は橘逸勢に書かせた。

　当時、空海大師は既に日本仏教真言宗の開祖になり、社会地位は非常に高い。比較的に低い社会地位に居る橘逸勢は、嵯峨天皇、空海大師と並べて門額を書いたことから、彼の書道はよほど評価されたことが伺

える。

　しかし、承和9年（842）、嵯峨太上天皇葬儀の翌日、橘逸勢は皇位継承をめぐる政治紛争に巻き込まれ、謀反の罪を問われて伊豆半島に流される。

　8月13日、伊豆へ配流の途中、重病にかかった橘逸勢は遠江国板築駅で病没した。

　噂によれば、橘逸勢が配流された時から、彼の一人娘は昼夜を兼ねて後を追っていた。父が没後、その娘は髪を切って出家し、お墓の近くに草庵を営み菩提を弔い続けた。また、その娘が父の遺体を背負って都に戻ったという説もある。とにかく、孝行娘の妙沙尼の話が広く伝わり、人々を感動させた。嘉祥3年（850）、ようやく橘逸勢を故郷に帰葬

させることができた。

　仁寿3年（853）、文徳天皇は橘逸勢の名誉と橘の本名を回復させた
上に、従四位下が贈位された。

　現在、世に残した橘逸勢の真跡とされるものは、『伊都内親王願文』
しかない。この作品の内容は伊都親王宛ての願文である。書風は今まで
のと違い、李北海に似ていながら独特の格調があり、運筆の方法は「二
王」（中国書家の王羲之、王献之）を受け継いだが、作品全体の趣は唐
の人に相似している。雄渾な筆跡と大らかな気迫は、二王のやや婉曲な
書風を革新したともいえる。

One of Japan's Three Great Calligraphers

—Tachibana no Hayanari

Tachibana no Hayanari (782—842) was a prominent calligrapher in the Heian period (794—1185) of Japan. He, Master Kūkai, and Emperor Saga, were widely known as the Sanpitsu (Three Great Brushes) . Tachibana no Hayanari was born into a prestigious family. His great–grandfather Tachibana no Moroe served as Sadaijin (Minister of the Left) in the Nara period. His grandfather was Tachibana no Naramaro, and his father was Tachibana no Irii. Tachibana no Irii had two daughters, who were both appointed as Nyogo (rank of court lady) of Emperor Kanmu (reigned 781—806) . Tachibana no Hayanari was the third child to his parents.

In the twenty–third year of the Enryaku era (804) , Tachibana no Hayanari, together with Master Kūkai, went to Tang China with a mission. They both spent a period of time at Fuzhou Kaiyuan Temple. During his stay in China, Tachibana no Hayanari learned guqin (a plucked seven–string Chinese musical instrument) and calligraphy, in addition to Chinese language. He devoted himself to the study of the works of the great Chinese calligrapher Li Beihai and the great writer Liu Zongyuan. He admired Liu's poems and articles so much that he even paid a visit to Liu's residence for advice.

Among the three great Japanese calligraphers, Tachibana no Hayanari was the best at imitating the style of Tang calligraphy. His profound knowledge in Chinese culture and his casual and elegant bearing were literally no different from the cultural elites in the Tang dynasty. Marveled at his extraordinary talents, the Tang people affectionately hailed him as "Ju Xiucai" (Xiucai, literally "outstanding ability or talent").

In the eighth month of the first year of the Daido era（806）under Emperor Heizei's reign, Tachibana no Hayanari and Master Kūkai returned to Japan on the ship of Takashina no Tonari.

Japanese students, upon their return from studying in China, would all be arranged by the Japanese Imperial Court to work in politics, education, medicine, criminal law, arts or other sectors. However, Tachibana no Hayanari's political career did not fare well after his return, largely due to his disposition. According to *Shoku Nihon Kōki*, a Japanese history text, Tachibana no Hayanari was "dissolute in conduct and ignorant of social norms."

In the seventh year of the Jōwa era（840）, he was appointed as the Provisional Governor of Tajima Province with a low government position.

However, his low political rank did not affect his reputation a bit as an eminent calligrapher. In 818, Emperor Saga personally inscribed words on the plaques of the three gates in the east of the Heian Palace; Master Kūkai inscribed words on the plaques of the three gates in the south; and those of the three gates in the north were inscribed by Tachibana no Hayanari.

By then, as the founder of Japanese Shingon Buddhism, Master Kūkai had an extremely high social status. The fact that Tachibana no Hayanari could join the rank of Emperor Saga and Master Kūkai in inscribing words on the plaques in the Heian Palace indicates his calligraphy skills won undivided admiration at that time.

In the ninth year of the Jōwa era（842）under Emperor Ninmyō's reign, the day after Emperor Saga died, Tachibana no Hayanari got involved in a political riot related to the succession of the throne. Consequently, he was convicted of rebellion and banished to the Izu Peninsula.

On the thirteenth day of the eighth month of the same year, on his way to exile, serious illness caused Tachibana no Hayanari to die in a small inn in Tōtōmi Province.

It is said that his only daughter followed him day and night since the beginning of his exile. After Tachibana no Hayanari's death, she had her hair cut to become a nun, and built a Buddhist nunnery in the vicinity of her father's tomb. There is another narrative, saying that she took her father's body back to the capital. In any case, the story of Tachibana no Hayanari's good daughter was widely circulated, which moved many people. Finally, in the third year of the Kashō era (850) , Tachibana no Hayanari's tomb was relocated to his hometown.

In the third year of the Ninju era (853) , Emperor Montoku restored his reputation and his surname, and conferred upon him the posthumous title of Jushiige (Junior Fourth Rank, Lower Grade) .

The only verified calligraphy work of Tachibana no Hayanari remaining in the world is *Ito Naishin'no Ganmon* (literally Princess Ito's Prayer) . The style of this work was strikingly similar to Li Beihai's, but it was also unique in its own. The way he wrote resembled that of Wang Xizhi and Wang Xianzhi, the two great calligraphers in ancient China. However, the writing style of the work was much closer to that of the calligraphy works in the Tang dynasty. The use of thick brushstrokes and the formidable momentum represented an innovation of the calligraphy styles of Wang Xizhi and Wang Xianzhi, while showing a certain degree of gracefulness.

日本东大寺重建圣人

——重源上人

重源上人，日本中世纪初期（平安末期至镰仓前期）高僧。他前后三次到中国（当时的南宋）求学，学习佛法和建筑技术，在日本佛教界被尊称为"入唐三度圣人重源"，又因为他重建了日本著名寺院东大寺，又被尊称为"东大寺劝进圣人重源"。

根据日本学者木宫泰彦所著《中日交通史》等史料，重源上人曾到福州开元寺和东禅寺，并将福州开元寺刊刻的《毗卢大藏经》和东禅寺刊刻

的《崇宁大藏经》（合称福州藏）带回日本。

在重建东大寺的时候，重源上人还主持重建了著名的东大寺大佛，这尊佛像的头像、坐姿、衣纹褶皱等，与福州开元寺的大铁佛有诸多相似处，让人不禁联想到当年重源上人在开元寺仰望大铁佛的情景。

在东大寺所收藏的宋版《福州藏》中，有《般若心经》并《般若心经诰谋抄》各一帖，中有墨书"奉渡日本国僧重源"八个字，可见重源上人从福州带回大藏经的恭敬和欣喜。

根据《俊乘房重源史料集成》等资料，重源于保安二年（1121）生于京都，俗名重定，其父为当时的没落贵族纪季重。长承二年（1133），纪重定十三岁时，在京都山科的醍醐寺出家，僧名重源，又叫"俊乘房"，开始修行真言密教。之后，他又到日本净土宗开山祖师法然上人处学习。

中国的宋代时期，经济、文化非常繁荣，政府鼓励与周边国家进行贸易，日本武士政权也一改前代锁国政策，鼓励海外贸易，中日两国贸易频繁。很多日本僧侣通过贸易商船入宋，南宋中叶以后日本僧人来华日益增多，知其姓名者就有120余人。

特别值得一提的是，当时，在重商政策推动下，福建商帮大大扩展了商业活动空间，这一时期福建港口的国内外航线也相继得到开辟，港口已由三国两晋南北朝时以军事活动为主要目的的军运型港口，逐渐转变成为地方经济服务的贸易港口。在商人商业贸易的推动下，福建与各国的经济、文化交流也逐渐频繁起来。当时，福州开元寺和东禅寺都刊刻了《大藏经》，日本的寺院对福州的宋版《大藏经》十分喜爱，一些有心来华求法的日本僧人，纷纷到福州来。

仁安二年（1167）重源上人首次到中国（当时的南宋）求学。他前后入宋三次，到了福州开元寺和东禅寺、山西五台山、宁波阿育王寺等地，学习佛法和建筑技术。重源上人回国后主持建造的寺院大多借鉴中国的建筑风格，他还邀请南宋建筑专家陈和卿到日本指导和协助建设。

奈良东大寺是世界文化遗产，又称大华严寺，是日本寺院的总寺，752 年圣武天皇为了祀奉大佛而建，在日本有着非常特殊的地位，中国唐代高僧鉴真大师曾在这里向圣武太上皇等僧俗授戒。当年，22 岁空海的大师就是因为在东大寺戒坛院正式受戒成为一名官僧，才有机会获准以留学僧的身份渡唐求法。空海大师回国后创立真言宗，宗风大振，后来他曾兼任东大寺别当，统辖一寺僧职，补大僧正位。

1180 年由于平重衡发起战争，放火烧毁了东大寺。重源上人被朝廷任命为"大劝进"，全面负责重建东大寺的工作。

1181 年，当时已 61 岁的重源不顾年迈，游历日本各地，劝募重建资金，他的努力得到了平民、贵族以及朝廷、幕府的支持。

　　1185 年（日本文治元年，南宋淳熙十二年）八月二十八日举行了盛大的佛像开眼供养仪式，不仅当时的天皇以及诸朝臣参加了仪式，幕府将军源赖朝也率领数万骑关东武士集体进京参加仪式，还有来自中国、印度和日本本地的共 1 万多名僧众同念一本佛经。

　　东大寺历时 25 年完成了重建。建久六年（1195）大佛殿落成时，举行了规模宏大的千僧供养仪式。

　　如今东大寺被列入世界文化遗产，寺内的大佛殿是世界上最大的木造古建筑，殿内供奉着卢舍那佛，是世界上最大的青铜佛像。

　　"大佛样"是重源上人在中国福建沿海一带学习，然后传到日本的建筑技术与样式，这一样式用于当年东大寺大佛殿的再建。近年来，日本建筑史家称之为"大佛样技法"。

　　现存的兵库县净土寺净土堂、奈良东大寺南大门和开山堂都是大佛样的代表作。镰仓时代，由入宋日僧荣西、道元和南宋蜀僧兰溪道隆等人传入日本的另一种建筑技术与样式，则被称为"禅宗样"，它是根据南宋江浙地区"五山十刹"等禅宗重要寺院模式而建的。

　　重源上人入宋凡三次，除经卷外，还携回其他物品。如奉安于高野山的中国所雕之观音、势至像等。他还受法然上人之托，带回净土五祖昙鸾、道绰、善导、怀感、少康的画像。

日本東大寺再興聖人

——重源上人

　　重源上人，日本中世紀初期（平安末期から鎌倉前期）の高僧。中国（南宋）を 3 度訪れて、仏法や建築技術を習得したことから、日本仏教界で「入唐三度聖人重源」と尊称される。また、日本東大寺を再建したことから、「東大寺勧進聖人重源」とも尊称される。

　　日本学者木宮泰彦の著書『中日交通史』などの資料によると、重源上人は福州開元寺と東禅寺を訪れて、福州開元寺が彫刻印刷した『毘盧大蔵経』と東禅寺が彫刻印刷した『崇寧大蔵経』（福州蔵と併称）を日本に持ち帰った。

　　東大寺再建の際、重源上人は有名な東大寺大仏の建造に携わっていた。仏像の顔、座り方、衣紋のしわなどは、福州開元寺の大鉄仏によく似ていて、重源上人は開元寺で大鉄仏を仰ぎ見る光景を思わず連想させられる。

　　東大寺が収蔵する宋代の『福州蔵』の中に、『般若心経』及び『般若心経詰謀抄』がそれぞれ一つあり、そこに墨で書いてある「奉渡日本国僧重源」という八つの文字が見られる。福州から大蔵経を持ってきた時、重源上人はいかに謹んで喜ぶかは伺えることだろう。

　　『俊乗房重源史料集成』などの資料により、重源は保安二年（1121）
京都に生まれて、俗名は重定、没落貴族紀季重の子である。長承 2 年
（1133）、13 歳の紀重定は京都山科の醍醐寺に入り出家し、僧名は重源、
「俊乗房」とも称し、真言密教を修行し始める。のち、日本浄土宗開祖
の法然上人の門に入った。

　　中国宋の時代、経済と文化は盛んに発展し、政府は周辺諸国との貿
易を推奨している。日本の武士政権も前代の鎖国政策を一変させ、海外
貿易を推奨している。中日間の貿易は盛んに行われた。大勢の日本僧侶
が貿易商船に乗って宋に入り、南宋中期以降はその数を増して、名前が
記載された者だけで 120 人余りいた。

　　特に、商業を重視する政策が推進されるとともに、福建の商人団体
は商業活動の範囲を大幅に拡大した。福建港で国内外航路が続々と開
かれて、港は三国両晋南北朝時代の軍事活動を主要目的とする軍用港か
ら、地方経済を振興するための貿易港に変わりつつある。商業貿易が進

むとともに、福建は各国との経済・文化交流も徐々に頻繁に行っていた。当時、福州開元寺と東禅寺が『大蔵経』を彫刻印刷した。日本の寺院は宋代福州の『大蔵経』に興味を持つため、中国に来て求法する僧侶たちは続々と福州を訪れていた。

仁安2年（1167）、重源上人は初めて中国（当時の南宋）に渡った。前後3度宋に入り、福州の開元寺と東禅寺、山西五台山、寧波阿育王寺などを訪れて、仏法や建築技術を習得した。重源上人は帰国後建造された寺院は、中国の建築様式の影響が強いほうである。また、南宋建築家の陳和卿を日本に招聘して、大仏鋳造の指導と協力に当たっている。

奈良東大寺は世界文化遺産であり、大華厳寺とも称せられ、日本華厳宗の大本山である。752年に聖武天皇が開眼供養のために造営され、日本では非常に特別な地位を持っている。中国唐代高僧の鑑真和尚はここで聖武上皇らに戒を授けたことがある。当時22歳の空海大師も東大寺戒壇院で授戒を受けて官僧になり、留学僧の身分で唐に渡ることができた。空海大師は帰国後、真言宗を開き、仏法が勢いよく広がった。のち、東大寺別当を兼任し、寺の僧職を統轄し、大僧正位を追贈られた。

1180年、平重衡による戦争を起こし、東大寺の大部分を焼失した。重源上人は勅命によって「大勧進」に任命され、東大寺の再興に全面的に取り組んでいた。

1181年、61歳の重源は老境を顧みず、再建資金を募集するために、日本各地を奔走した。その努力によって平民、貴族、朝廷、幕府の支持を獲得した。

　　1185 年（日本文治元年、南宋淳熙 12 年）8 月 28 日、大仏開眼供養が盛大に行われ、当時の天皇及び諸大臣が式に参加した。幕府将軍の源頼朝も数万騎の関東武士を率いて上京して参列していた。また、中国やインド、日本各地から 1 万人あまりの僧侶や信者が参加して一斉に読経していた。

　　東大寺の再建は 25 年を経て完成した。建久 6 年（1195）、大仏殿が落慶した時、千僧供養会が盛大に執り行われた。

　　今、東大寺は世界遺産リストに登録されている。境内の大仏殿は世界最大級の木造建築であり、世界最大級の青銅仏像の盧舎那仏坐像が殿内に鎮座している。

　　「大仏様」とは、重源上人が中国福建沿岸部で習得し、日本に伝わってきた建築技術と様式である。この様式は、当時東大寺大仏殿の再建

に用いられていた。近年、日本建築史学者はそれを「大仏様技法」と呼んでいる。

　現存している兵庫県浄土寺の浄土堂、奈良東大寺の南大門と開山堂は大仏様の代表作である。また、鎌倉時代に、入宋僧の栄西、道元、そして南宋四川出身の禅僧蘭渓道隆らが日本に伝わってきたもう一つの建築技術・様式は「禅宗様」と呼ばれ、南宋江蘇省、浙江省地域の「五山十刹」など重要な禅寺の様式を模倣して構築された。

　重源上人は三回も入宋し、仏教経巻のほか、高野山に祀られている中国で彫刻された観音・勢至菩薩像などの物品を持ち帰った。また、法然上人に託されて、浄土五祖と呼ばれる曇鸞・道綽・善導・懐感・少康の画像を持ち帰った。

Daikanjin of Tōdaiji Temple in Japan

—Great Monk Chōgen

Chōgen（1121—1206）was a great Buddhist monk in early Medieval Japan （from the late Heian period to the early Kamakura period）. He made three trips to China altogether during the Southern Song dynasty（1127—1279）to study Buddhism and architecture. Later, he rebuilt the famous temple Tōdaiji（Great Eastern Temple）in Japan. Thus, he was honored as the Great Monk Who Made Three Pilgrimages to China and the Great Kanjin of Tōdaiji Temple by Japanese Buddhist monks.

During his trips to China, Chōgen visited the Kaiyuan Temple and the Dongchan Temple in Fuzhou, Fujian Province and brought back to Japan the Pilu Tripitaka and the Chongning Tripitaka（collectively called the Fuzhou Tripitaka）printed by the Kaiyuan Temple and the Dongchan Temple respectively, according to historical records such as *The* History of Sino-Japanese Cultural Exchanges by Japanese scholar Yasuhiko Kimiya.

During the rebuilding of Tōdaiji Temple, Chōgen also presided over the reconstruction of the famous Great Buddha statue at Tōdaiji Temple. The statue bears many similarities to the iron Great Buddha at Fuzhou Kaiyuan Temple in their heads, sitting positions and folds of their robes, which are strongly reminiscent of the days when Chōgen looked up at the Great Buddha at Fuzhou Kaiyuan Temple.

The printed Fuzhou Tripitaka of the Song edition was kept at Tōdaiji Temple. In this book, the sentence "Monk Chōgen Sent to China by the Japanese Imperial Court" was written in ink in both the *Heart of Prajna Paramita Sutra* and the *Annotated Heart of Prajna Paramita Sutra*, which shows the piety and joy of Chōgen when he brought back the Tripitaka from Fuzhou.

The *Historical Records Collection on Shunjōbō Chōgen* and other documentation show that Chōgen was born into the fallen noble Ki clan as the son of Ki no Sueshige in Kyoto in the second year of the Hōan era (1121) and was formerly named Ki no Shigesada. In the second year of the Chōshō era (1133) , at the age of 13, he was initiated into religious life at Daigoji Temple in Kyoto and was given the religious name of Chōgen, or Shunjōbō Chōgen. Then he began to study Shingon Esoteric Buddhism there. Later, Chōgen studied under the monk Hōnen, founder of the first independent branch of Japanese Pure Land Buddhism called Jōdo–shū.

During the Song dynasty, the economy and culture flourished in China. The Song government encouraged the overseas trade and the Japanese Samurai regime also abandoned its previous closed–door policy. As mutual trade increased between China and Japan, many Japanese monks traveled to China by trading ships. After the middle of the Southern Song dynasty, more and more

Japanese monks came to China, 120 of whom have their names recorded.

It is particularly worth mentioning that fueled by the Song government's focus on commerce, the chamber of commerce in Fujian Province greatly expanded the business, and new domestic and overseas sea routes were opened up. The once–military port which dated back to the Three Kingdoms period (220—280) of China had been gradually turned into a trading port serving the local economy. Driven by the trade, both economic and cultural exchanges between Fujian Province and other countries became more frequent. At that time, both Fuzhou Kaiyuan Temple and Fuzhou Dongchan Temple engraved the Tripitaka which attracted many Japanese monks. That's why some Japanese monks who wanted to study Buddhism in China chose to come to Fuzhou.

In the second year of the Nin'an era (1167), Chōgen traveled to China for the first time. He made three trips to China altogether during the Southern Song dynasty to study Buddhism and architecture at various places, including the Kaiyuan Temple and the Dongchan Temple in Fuzhou, Mount Wutai in Shanxi Province, and the King Ashoka Temple in Ningbo. After Chōgen returned to Japan, most of the temples of which he presided over the construction were heavily influenced by Chinese architecture. He also invited Chen Heqing, a Chinese architect of the Southern Song dynasty, to Japan to provide guidance and assistance on the reconstruction.

As the headquarter of the Kegon sect of Buddhism, Tōdaiji Temple in Nara is a listed UNESCO World Heritage Site and was once the most powerful temple in Japan. It was built by the Japanese Emperor Shōmu to worship the Great Buddha and was completed in 752. Tōdaiji Temple has a very special status in Japan. It was the place where Chinese monk Jianzhen in the Tang dynasty (618—907) ordained Japanese monks and laymen, including Emperor Shōmu. At that time, 22–year–old Kūkai was ordained as an official monk at the ordination platform at Tōdaiji Temple so that he was allowed by the Japanese Imperial Court to travel to China to study Buddhism. After he returned to Japan, Kūkai founded the Japanese Shingon Buddhism. Later, he was appointed as bettō (supervisor) at Tōdaiji Temple, in charge of all the monk there, and was granted the rank of Gon–Daisojo (the provisional highest position of a Buddhist sect, upper grade) .

In 1180, Tōdaiji Temple was burned down due to the war initiated by Taira no Shigehira. Chōgen was appointed by the Japanese Imperial Court as Great

Kanjin and was fully responsible for the reconstruction of Tōdaiji Temple.

In 1181, at age 61, Chōgen traveled around Japan to solicit donations for the reconstruction of Tōdaiji Temple. His efforts were supported by commoners, nobles, the imperial court and the shōgunate (the feudal military government of Japan) .

On the twenty-eighth day of the eighth month of the first year of Bunji era, an official "eye-opening" ceremony of the Great Buddha statue was held at Tōdaiji Temple in Nara. Japanese Emperor, government officials, and the Shōgun Minamoto no Yoritomo with his army, tens of thousands of samurai riding horses from the Kanto region, attended the ceremony. There were more than 10,000 monks from China, India and Japan chanting a same Buddhist scripture.

It took 25 years to rebuild Tōdaiji Temple. In the sixth year of Kenkyū era (1195) , when the Great Buddha Hall was completed, a grand ceremony was held to give alms to thousands of monks.

Tōdaiji Temple is now a listed World Heritage Site. Its Great Buddha Hall is the largest ancient wooden structure in the world and houses an immense statue of Vairocana Buddha, which is the world's largest bronze Buddha statue.

The Great Buddha style is an architectural design that Chōgen learned along the coast of Fujian Province, China, and then was introduced to Japan. This style was used in the reconstruction of the Great Buddha hall. The style has been called "Daibutsu-yo" by Japanese architectural historians.

The Jōdo–do Hall of Jōdoji Temple in Hyōgo Prefecture, the Great South Gate and the Kaisando Hall of Tōdaiji Temple are all classic examples of Daibutsu–yo architecture. Zenshūyo (Zen style) , also known as the Chinese Style (karayō) , is another architectural style introduced to Japan during the Kamakura period by Japanese monks such as Eisai and Dōgen and Chinese monk Lanxi Daolong from the Shu (now Sichuan Province) . The style was developed based on the important Chan (Zen) Buddhist temples including the Five Mountains and Ten Monasteries in the Jiangnan area.

Chōgen sailed to China for three times altogether, and brought back to Japan many items, including scriptures and Avalokiteshvara (Guanyin) and Mahāsthāmaprāpta statues carved by Chinese sculptors which are now placed at Mount Kōya. He also brought back portraits of the five promoters of the Pure Land Buddhism, namely Tanluan, Daochuo, Shandao, Huaigan, and Shaokang, at the request of Monk Hōnen.

日本律宗戒光寺派开山祖师

——昙照律师

公元1214年，在重源上人首次入宋近五十年后，日本又有昙照律师来华，并到福州开元寺求法。

昙照律师（1187—1259），日本律宗名僧，戒光寺派开山祖师，名净业，字法忍，山城人，昙照律师早年出家，先在园城寺学显密二教，后游学南都。

鉴真大师为日本律宗之祖。在奈良时代的孝谦天皇时，因为中国唐代高僧鉴真到日本传法，日本律宗一时大为兴盛。到了平安时代，律宗渐次

萎靡不振，法脉殆危。当时僧侣，多有堕落之风。为了传习律法、重振日本律宗，很多日本僧侣入宋学律。

根据日本学者木宫泰彦所著《中日交通史》等资料，1214 年（日本建保二年，宋宁宗嘉定七年），昙照律师入宋求法。他师从铁翁守一学律，铁翁守一是传承中国律宗中兴祖师元照律师法脉的高僧。昙照律师遍游各州县，探求教律。据日本高僧传记载，由于他修行的成就，宋理宗曾赐其"忍律法师"之称号。

昙照律师曾长住福州开元寺，并得到了福州开元寺刊刻的《毗卢大藏经》。

现存的日本大藏经古籍刻本，几乎均含有福州开元寺版《毗卢藏》。

中国自北宋以后，随着刻版技术与印刷术的发展，大规模刻印大藏经的工程，成为宋代佛教繁荣的一个重要标志。两宋出现的著名大藏经计有五种，其中两种出自福州，即福州东禅寺刻印的《崇宁万寿藏》和福州开元寺刻印的《毗卢藏》。

福州开元寺雕版《毗卢藏》始自北宋末年，至南宋初年止，前后历时近 50 年，后来又有补刻，在中国佛教刻经史上具有重要的历史意义。《毗卢藏》的雕刻，历经福州开元寺的七任住持，显示了当年福州开元寺作为闽中大寺的地位和影响力。

据日本学者村上专精所著的《日本佛教史纲》、望月信亨所著的《中国净土教理史》等资料，昙照律师在华留学十四年后，于安贞二年（1228）回国，在京都兴建戒光寺，弘扬律法，大兴律宗。此后，戒光寺和俊芿律师创立的泉涌寺并立，成为京都的两大律庭。

宋绍定六年（1233）他把戒光寺托付给高徒，自己二度入宋学习，这次在华八年。他从铁翁守一增受戒法，研究律藏。守一曾为其撰写《重受戒文》，以示其律学之深意。

他于仁治二年（1241）回国，在归国时又带回大量佛像、宋版《福州藏》，并在筑紫创立西林寺，在洛东开创东林寺。

此后，昙照律师在这些寺中宣扬戒法，弘传元照律师一系的律学。晚年他也同元照律师一样，归心净土，专修念佛。

昙照律师正元元年（1259）圆寂，年七十三岁。

日本律宗戒光寺派の開祖

——曇照律師

　　西暦 1214 年、重源上人は初めて入宋してから五十年が経った。続いて、曇照律師は宋に入り、福州開元時で求法していた。

　　曇照律師（ 1187—1259 ）、日本律宗の名僧、戒光寺派の開祖、名は浄業、字は法忍、山城の出身である。

　　曇照律師は若い時に出家し、園城寺で顕密二教を学んだ後、南部を遊学していた。

　　鑑真和上は日本における律宗の開祖である。奈良時代孝謙天皇が在位した時、中国唐代の高僧鑑真が渡日して戒律を伝え、日本の律宗は一時盛んに発展した。平安時代になると、律宗は次第に不振になり、法脈は危ない境地に陥った。当時、多くの僧侶は堕落している。律法を伝習して日本の律宗を復興させるために、多くの日本僧侶は宋に行き、戒律を勉強した。

　　日本学者木宮泰彦の著書『中日交通史』などの資料によると、1214年（日本建保 2 年、宋寧宗嘉定 7 年）、曇照律師は入宋求法し、鉄翁守一に師事して戒律を学ぶ。鉄翁守一は中国律宗中興祖師である元照律師の法脈を受け継いだ高僧である。曇照律師は各州・県を遍歴し、教

法・戒律を求めいる。日本高僧伝によると、彼の修行が成就することから、宋の理宗皇帝より「忍律法師」の号を贈られる。

　　曇照律師は福州開元寺に長期に滞在したことがあり、福州開元寺が彫刻印刷した『毘盧大蔵経』を取得した。

　　現存している日本大蔵経の古籍刻本は、ほとんど福州開元寺版の『毘盧大蔵経』が含まれている。

　　北宋以降、中国は彫刻と印刷技術が発展するとともに、大蔵経を大規模に彫刻印刷し、宋代仏教繁盛の重要なシンボルの一つになる。北宋と南宋時代に現れた著名な大蔵経は合わせて五種類あり、その二種類は福州からであり、即ち福州東禅寺が彫刻印刷した『崇寧大蔵経』と福州開元寺が彫刻印刷した『毘盧大蔵経』となる。

　　福州開元寺版の『毘盧大蔵経』は北宋末期から南宋初期にかけて、前後50年かかって作成され、その後また補充作業が行われ、中国仏教経典刊刻の歴史の中で重要な意義を持っている。『毘盧大蔵経』の彫刻は、福州開元寺前後七代の住職を経て完成し、当時福州開元寺が福建省の大寺としての地位と影響力を表している。

　　日本学者村上専精の著書『日本仏教史綱』や望月信亨の著書『中国浄土教理史』などの資料によると、曇照律師は中国で14年間も留学し、安貞2年（1228）に帰朝した後、京都で戒光寺を創建して、律法を伝え、律宗を振興させた。のち、戒光寺は俊芿（しゅんじょう）律師の創立した泉涌寺と並べて京都の律宗二大寺になる。

　　宋の紹定6年（1233）、曇照律師は戒光寺を高弟に託して、再び宋

に渡る。今度は8年も宋に滞在し、鉄翁守一より戒を受け、律蔵を研究した。守一がそのために『重受戒文』を書き、奥深い律学の造詣を評価した。

仁治2年（1241）、曇照律師は帰朝し、大量の仏像と宋版の『福州蔵』を持ち帰った上に、筑紫で西林寺を創建し、洛東で東林寺を創建した。

　　その後、曇照律師はこれらの寺で戒を伝え、元照律師法脈の律学を伝えた。晩年の彼は、元照律師と同じく浄土に専念し、専修念仏をした。

　　正元元年（1259）、曇照律師は円寂、享年73歳。

Founder of Kaikouji Temple in Japan

一Risshū Monk Donsho Ninritsu

In 1214, nearly fifty years after the Japanese great monk Chōgen's first visit to China during the Song dynasty, the Japanese Risshū monk Donsho Ninritsu journeyed to China and came to Fuzhou Kaiyuan Temple for the study of Risshū.

Donsho Ninritsu（1187—1259）was a famous monk of Risshū（also Ritsu school, one of the six schools of Nara Buddhism in Japan）and the founder of Kaikouji Temple. Born in Yamashiro, Donsho Ninritsu, who was given the secular name Jogo and the courtesy name Bonin, became a monk in his early years. He first studied Exoteric and Esoteric Buddhism at Onjōji Temple and later embarked on a study tour in Nara（Nanto, the southern capital）.

The Chinese great monk Jianzhen in the Tang dynasty was the founder of Risshū in Japan. During the reign of Empress Kōken in the Nara period, Risshū flourished in Japan because Jianzhen sailed there to preach Buddhism. However, during the Heian period, Risshū was in gradual decay and its Dharma transmission was in danger. At that time, many Risshū monks committed acts of misconduct. In order to preach and revitalize Risshū in Japan, many Japanese monks came to China during the Song dynasty.

In the second year of the Kenpo era or the seventh year of the Jiading era

（1214）, Donsho Ninritsu journeyed to Song China to study Risshū, according

to historical records such as *The* History of Sino-Japanese Cultural Exchanges

by Japanese scholar Yasuhiko Kimiya. He studied under the famous Risshū

monk Shouyi, who was one of the successors in the Risshū monk Yuanzhao's

（key promoter of Risshū revitalization）lineage. Later Donsho Ninritsu traveled

around China for the understanding of the Buddhist doctrines. He was bestowed

the title of "Risshū Master" by Emperor Lizong of the Song dynasty due to his

profound understanding of Risshū, according to *Memoirs of Japanese Eminent*

Monks.

During his stay in China, Donsho Ninritsu once lived at Fuzhou Kaiyuan

Temple for a long time and obtained the Pilu Tripitaka engraved by the temple.

This edition of the Pilu Tripitaka could be found in almost all the existing

engraved Tripitakas in Japan.

With the development of engraving and printing technology in the Northern

Song dynasty, large-scale engraving and printing projects of the Tripitaka had

emerged, which represented an important sign of the prosperity of Buddhism

in the Song dynasty. There were five well-known editions of the Tripitaka

engraved during the Song dynasty, two of which were engraved in Fuzhou,

namely the Pilu Tripitaka by Fuzhou Kaiyuan Temple and the Chongning

Tripitaka by Fuzhou Dongchan Temple（collectively called the Fuzhou

Tripitaka) .

From the end of the Northern Song dynasty to the beginning of the Southern Song dynasty, it took around 50 years for Fuzhou Kaiyuan Temple to engrave the Pilu Tripitaka and some contents were added later. The engraving project is of significant importance in the history of China's engraved Buddhist scriptures and was presided over by seven successive abbots of Fuzhou Kaiyuan Temple, which shows the status and influence of this major temple in central Fujian Province.

After 14 years of study in China, Donsho Ninritsu returned to Japan in the second year of the Antei era (1228) and founded Kaikouji Temple in Kyoto to preach and revitalize Risshū, according to historical records including *History of Buddhism in Japan* by Japanese scholar Senshō Murakami and *Pure Land Buddhism in China: A Doctrinal History* by Shinkō Mochizuki. Since then, Kaikouji Temple and Sennyūji Temple which was founded by the Risshū monk Shunjō, became the two main Risshū temples in Kyoto.

In the first year of the Tenpuku era or the sixth year of the Shaoding era (1233) , Donsho Ninritsu entrusted Kaikouji Temple to his disciples and made a second trip to China for the purpose of studying Risshū. During the next eight years, he took the precepts from the Risshū monk Shouyi and studied the Vinaya Pitaka. Monk Shouyi once wrote *Retaking the Precepts* for Donsho Ninritsu to show his profound understanding of Risshū.

In the second year of the Ninji era (1241) , Donsho Ninritsu brought back to Japan a large number of Buddha statues and the Fuzhou Tripitaka of the Song edition. Then he founded two temples in Japan, namely, the Sairinji Temple in Tsukushi Province and the Torinji Temple in eastern Kyoto.

Since then, Donsho Ninritsu preached the Buddhist precepts in these temples, and propagated the Buddhist teachings of Yuanzhao's lineage. In his later years, like Yuanzhao, he also immersed himself in the world of Buddhism.

Donsho Ninritsu died in the first year of the Shōgen era at the age of 73.

日本诗僧

——庆政上人

昙照律师来华三年后，公元 1217 年，日本诗僧庆政上人踏上来华求法之路，他也曾来到福州开元寺，并带回《毗卢藏》。

庆政上人，自号胜月，又号证月，出身于日本著名贵族九条氏之家，是摄政太政大臣九条良经长子，弟弟是被称为"光明峰寺关白"的权臣藤原道家，侄子是镰仓幕府第四代将军藤原赖经。

庆政上人出家于近江园城寺，即圆珍大师所开创的天台宗寺门派大本山，是日本天台宗圆珍大师一脉的传人。庆政上人先后依止天台宗寺门派僧能舜、庆范、延朗等高僧学习天台教义，又随日本华严宗中兴之祖明惠上人修学，后栖隐京都西山修行。

庆政上人能文善诗，尤精于和歌，《续古今和歌集》中收有其诗 22 首；又著有《闲居友》，是日本著名的佛教说话集。庆政上人与被后世誉为"日本华严宗中兴之祖"的明惠上人是至交。明惠上人是一位生涯颇具传奇色彩的高僧，他自幼父母双亡，自誓以佛陀为慈父。明惠上人曾发愿要前往印度朝圣，甚至为此制订了周密计划，但因为身体原因终未能成行。

公元 1217 年，庆政上人受明惠上人之托，渡海来到中国。他曾著有

《证月上人渡唐日记》《漂到琉球国记》，记录他的行止见闻，可惜都已经
佚失。根据目前的资料，可以知道庆政上人曾先后在福建的泉州、福州
居留。

根据日本学者木宫泰彦所著的《日中文化交流史》、桥本进吉的《庆
政上人传考》等资料，1218 年，庆政上人归国时，将福州开元寺版《毗卢
藏》与福州东禅寺版《崇宁藏》带回。

庆政上人带回的福州版《大藏经》，现收藏于日本宫内厅图书馆。在
所藏的《大涅槃经》卷第三十三的版心有"日本国僧庆政 舍"的刊记，
《大方广佛华严经》卷二十三的版心中有"日本国僧庆政舍周正刀"的
刊记。

同书《大般涅槃经》卷第三十六的版心中有"日本国僧行一 舍版十

片"的刊记，另外《妙法莲华经》卷第七的版心中有"日本国比丘明仁 舍刊换"的刊记。至于"行一""明仁"，其事迹不明。据木宫泰彦的推测，行一、明仁当与庆政同时或随从庆政来到福州，且与带回的《大藏经》有关。

庆政上人还从泉州带回用波斯文写的文书。日本高山寺所藏的《波斯文书》题记云："此是南蕃文字也。南无释迦如来南无阿弥陀佛也，两三人到来舶上望书之。时大宋嘉定十年丁丑于泉州记之。""为送遣本朝辨和尚（高辨明惠上人），禅庵令书之，彼和尚殊芳印度之风故也。沙门庆政记之。"据专家考定，庆政上人带回的《波斯文书》是古阿拉伯文的诗歌集，是古阿拉伯文字遗留于东方的最早珍本。

庆政上人于公元 1263 年在京都西山创建了法华山寺，并举行了《一切经》（即大藏经）供养法会。五年后，庆政上人以八十岁高龄安详入寂。

福州版大藏经的输入，对日本的佛教事业和印刷事业起到了极大的推动作用，此后日本的各种佛书、汉籍开始仿刻出版，其版本样式，与福州版大藏经几乎一模一样。

日本詩僧

——慶政上人

　　曇照律師が中国に来てから三年後の西暦 1217 年、日本詩僧の慶政上人が中国へ求法の道を旅立った。彼も福州開元寺を訪れて、『毘盧大蔵経』を日本に持ち帰った。

　　慶政上人、勝月または証月と号す。日本有名な貴族九条家に生まれ、摂政・太政大臣九条良経の長男であり、「光明峯寺関白」と呼ばれる権臣藤原道家の兄にあたり、鎌倉幕府第四代将軍藤原頼経の伯父にあたる。

　　慶政上人は円珍大師が開いた天台宗寺門派大本山の近江園城寺で出家し、日本天台宗円珍大師の法脈を受け継いた人である。前後に天台宗寺門派高僧の能舜、慶範、延朗らに師事した上に、日本華厳宗中興の祖と称される明恵上人のもとへ参学した。のち、京都西山に隠居し、修行していた。

　　慶政上人は文学と詩歌に精通し、特に俳句が得意な人である。『続古今和歌集』以下の勅撰集に 22 首入集し、日本著名な仏教説話集『閑居友』をも完成した。慶政上人は「日本華厳宗中興の祖」と称される明恵上人と親交を結んだ。明恵上人は伝奇的な生涯を送った高僧であり、

幼い時から両親を亡くし、仏を慈父にすることを自ら誓った。明恵上人はインドへの聖地巡礼を誓願し、そのために周密な計画も立てましたが、身体の原因で実行することができなかった。

西暦 1217 年、慶政上人は明恵上人に託されて、宋に渡った。『証月上人渡唐日記』『漂到琉球国記』など遊歴見聞を記録した著書を書いたが、残念ながらみな散失した。現在の資料によって、慶政上人は前後福建省の泉州、福州に滞在していたことがわかる。

日本学者木宮泰彦の著書『日中文化交流史』や橋本進吉の著書『慶政上人伝考』などの資料によると、1218 年慶政上人が帰朝時、福州開元寺版『毘盧大蔵経』と福州東禅寺版『崇寧大蔵経』を持ち帰った。

慶政上人が持ち帰った福州版『大蔵経』は、現在日本宮内庁図書館に収蔵されている。所蔵の『大涅槃経』巻第三十三の版芯に「日本国僧慶政舎」の印記があり、『大方広仏華厳経』巻第二十三の版芯に「日本国僧慶政舎周正刀」の印記がある。

同じく『大般涅槃経』巻第三十六の版芯に「日本国僧行一舎版十片」の印記がある他、『妙法蓮華経』巻第七の版芯に「日本国比丘明仁舎刊換」の印記がある。なお、「行一」、「明仁」についての事績は不明である。行一、明仁が慶政と同時に、または慶政に就いて福州に到着したはずであり、それに慶政の持ち帰った『大蔵経』に関係があると木宮泰彦が推測している。

慶政上人はまた、泉州からペルシャ語の文書を日本に持ち帰った。日本高山寺所蔵の『紙本墨書南番文字』では、「此是南番文字也。南無

釋迦如來南無阿彌陀佛也、兩三人到來船上望書之。尔時大宋嘉定十年丁丑於泉洲記之。」や「爲送遺本朝弁和尚（高弁明惠上人）禪菴令書之、彼和尚殊芳印度之風故也。砂門慶政謹記之。」などが書いてある。専門家の考証によって、慶政上人が持ち帰った『紙本墨書南番文字』は、古代アラビア語の詩歌集であり、古代アラビア文字が東洋に残された最初の珍本である。

　　西暦 1263 年、慶政上人は京都西山に法華山寺を創建し、『一切経』（大蔵経のこと）を供養する法会を行った。五年後、慶政上人は 80 歳の高齢で入寂した。

　　福州版大蔵経の伝来は、日本の仏教及び印刷業を大いに促進した。その後、日本で各種の仏書や漢籍がそれを模倣して刻印出版された。その板本と様式はほとんど福州版大蔵経にそっくりである。

Japanese Monk—Poet

—Keisei

In 1217, three years after the Japanese Risshū monk Donsho Ninritsu's first visit to China, Keisei, the Japanese monk–poet, journeyed to China for the study of Buddhism. He also came to Fuzhou Kaiyuan Temple and brought back to Japan the Pilu Tripitaka.

Keisei, art name Syougetsu, was born into the famous noble family of Kujō in Japan as the eldest son of the Regent Yoshitsune Kujō. He was the elder brother of Michiie Kujō, or Fujiwara no Michiie, the powerful "Former Regent Lay–priest of Komyobuji Temple", and the uncle of Yoritsune Kujō, or Fujiwara no Yoritsune, the fourth shōgun (the military dictator of Japan) of the Kamakura shōgunate.

Keisei entered into a religious life at Onjōji Temple, the head temple of the Jimon School of Tendai Buddhism. The school was founded by Master Enchin. Keisei was one of the successors of Enchin's lineage. He first studied under the famous monks of Tendai Buddhism, including Noshun, Keihan, and Enrou. Then he studied under the monk Myōe, key promoter of the Kegon School of Japanese Buddhism. Later Keisei headed off to Nishiyama (western mountain) in Kyoto to practice Buddhism.

Keisei was good at writing articles and poems, especially waka (a type of poetry in classical Japanese literature) . 22 of his poems were collected in *Shokukokin Wakashū* (Poetry Anthology of Ancient and Modern Times Continued) . He was also the author of *Kankyo no Tomo* (A Companion in Solitude) , a famous Japanese Buddhist tales collection. Keisei developed a close relationship with Myōe, who was a legendary monk in Japan. Myōe lost both his parents when he was a child and swore to treat Buddha as his loving father. He wished to go on a pilgrimage to India, and even made a careful plan for it. However, he failed to make the journey due to health reasons.

In 1217, Keisei sailed to China at the request of Myōe. He wrote *Monk Syougetsu's Diaries of a Pilgrimage to Tang China* and *Hyoto Ryukyukoku ki* (Record of the Voyage to Ryukyu) , which depicts his experiences as a pilgrim. Unfortunately, the two books were lost. Historical records show that during his stay in China, Keisei once lived in Quanzhou and Fuzhou in Fujian Province.

In 1218, Keisei brought back to Japan the Pilu Tripitaka and the Chongning Tripitaka engraved by Fuzhou Kaiyuan Temple and Fuzhou Dongchan Temple respectively, according to historical records such as *The* History of Sino-Japanese Cultural Exchanges by Japanese scholar Yasuhiko Kimiya and *Biography of Master Keisei* by Shinkichi Hashimoto.

The two editions of the Tripitaka are now kept at the Archives and Mausolea Department of the Imperial Household Agency of Japan. On the hanshin, the fore-edge of a folded sheet, of the volume thirty-third of the *Nirvana Sutra*, it writes "Wooden tablet donated by Japanese monk Keisei"；and on the hanshin of the volume twenty-third of the *Avatamsaka Sutra*, it writes "Wooden tablet donated by Japanese monk Keisei. Scriptures engraved by Zhouzheng".

On the hanshin of the volume thirty-sixth of the *Nirvana Sutra*, it writes "Ten pieces of wooden tablets donated by Japanese monk Gyouich"；and on the hanshin of the volume seventh of the *Lotus Sutra*, it writes "Wooden tablets donated by Japanese monk Meijin". However, there were no more records about these two monks. According to Yasuhiko Kimiya, monk Gyouichi and monk Meijin might come to Fuzhou at the same time as Keisei, and be associated with the introduction of the two editions of the Tripitaka into Japan.

Keisei also brought back from Quanzhou some documents written in

Persian. The inscription in *Persian Documents* kept at Kouzanji Temple in Japan reads, "These documents were written in a foreign language. Chanting Nama Amitabha, two or three men came to the ship to have a look at the documents. Recorded in Quanzhou in 1217, or the 10th year of the Jiading era of the Southern Song dynasty." Also, there are sentences "The Buddhist monastery asked Keisei to write the inscription for Monk Myōe who wanted to learn more about the culture and Buddhism in India. Recorded by monk Keisei." According to experts, *Persian Documents* is a collection of poems written in old Arabic, which is the earliest extant old Arabic text found in the East.

In 1263, Keisei founded Hokkesanji Temple in Nishiyama, Kyoto, and held an almsgiving ceremony for the Complete Buddhist Canon. Five years later, Keisei died peacefully at the age of 80.

The introduction of the two editions of the Tripitaka engraved in Fuzhou has played an active part in promoting Buddhism and the printing industry in Japan. Since then, various Japanese Buddhist books and imported Chinese books in Japan were engraved and printed in the format of the Fuzhou Tripitaka.